2004 POETRY

ONCE UPON A RHYME

IMAGINATION FOR A NEW GENERATION

Northern Kent

Edited by Donna Samworth

 Young**Writers**

First published in Great Britain in 2004 by:
Young Writers
Remus House
Coltsfoot Drive
Peterborough
PE2 9JX
Telephone: 01733 890066
Website: www.youngwriters.co.uk

SB ISBN 1 84460 482 9

Foreword

Young Writers was established in 1991 and has been passionately devoted to the promotion of reading and writing in children and young adults ever since. The quest continues today. Young Writers remains as committed to engendering the fostering of burgeoning poetic and literary talent as ever.

This year's Young Writers competition has proven as vibrant and dynamic as ever and we are delighted to present a showcase of the best poetry from across the UK. Each poem has been carefully selected from a wealth of *Once Upon A Rhyme* entries before ultimately being published in this, our twelfth primary school poetry series.

Once again, we have been supremely impressed by the overall high quality of the entries we have received. The imagination, energy and creativity which has gone into each young writer's entry made choosing the best poems a challenging and often difficult but ultimately hugely rewarding task - the general high standard of the work submitted amply vindicating this opportunity to bring their poetry to a larger appreciative audience.

We sincerely hope you are pleased with our final selection and that you will enjoy *Once Upon A Rhyme Northern Kent* for many years to come.

Contents

Georgia Wilkinson (7)	17
Bethany Fleming (8)	18
Jessica Sheehan (7)	18
James Adamson (7)	19
Joshua Hannan (7)	19
Thomas Barton (8)	20

Chantry Primary School

Mamunur Rahman (9)	20
Sadia Khalid (10)	21
Holly Marchant (9)	21
Suleman Hussain (10)	22
Jade Sargun (9)	22
Natasha Khalid (9)	23
Charlie Webb (9)	23
Zubair Ashraf (8)	24
Sunil Sidhu (9)	24
Emma Alvis (9)	25
Klajdi Alikaj (9)	25
Charanjit Kaur Samra (10)	26
Jack Boyd (10)	26
Junaid Khalid (9)	27
Jaid Stevens (10)	27
Lisa Gardiner (10)	28
Robeni Ali (10)	28
Zoheb Ashraf (9)	29
Emma Fitchett (9)	30
Nisha Chowdury (10)	30
Elliott Granger (9)	31
Navjeet Singhsall (9)	31
Stacey Williams (10)	32

Cliffe Woods Primary School

Jack Fryer (10)	32
James Lewis (11)	33
Alisa Hanger (10)	33
Lewis Cook (10)	34
Jessica Reuter (9)	34
Natasha Tyson (10)	35
Rochelle Leslie (10)	35
Elise Pocock (10)	36

Convent Preparatory School

Katy Nutt (10)   57
Nyree MacTavish (10)   58

Elaine Primary School
Kelly Patterson (10)   58
Toni Reynolds (10)   59
Alicia Whyte (11)   59
Zoe Keating (11)   60
Ejatu Turay (11)   60
Stacie Thomas (10)   61
Jodie Southgate (10)   62

Hilltop Primary School
Lizzi Hill (11)   62
Yasmin Brown (10)   63

Holy Trinity CE School
Aimee Newberry (7)   63
Toni Ives (11)   64
Ikra Arshad (10)   64
Thomas Uings (10)   65
Laura Walton (7)   65
Michael Adeyemo (11)   66
Danica Bassoo (8)   66
Megan Pretious (7)   67
Natasha Savage (7)   67
Ranveer Kaur (8)   68
Mohamed Kamara (7)   68
Amandeep Balrow (8)   68
Coyes Nahar (7)   69
George Pitcher (7)   69
Christian Fialho (8)   70
Manisha Binning (8)   70
Sharanjit Kang (11)   71
Shanice Sutherland (7)   71
Jaye Presland (10)   72
Emily Smith (8)   72
Jake Bennett (11)   73
Prabhdeep Dulay (8)   73
Adam Bassoo (9)   74
Nafeesa Arshad (7)   74

Ajay Singh Bedesha (8)	75
Rima Khatun (7)	75
Lakhmi Halaith (10)	76
Liam Tillman (7)	76
Blessings Obideyi (7)	77
Rafet Karabel (70	77
Farida Tejan (10)	78
Kieran Beveridge (7)	78
Jasmin Elliott (10)	79
Jaskiran Kaur Sodhi (7)	79
Pavendeep Kallu (11)	80
Janet Amu (10)	80
Chantel Higglesden (7)	81
Noor Chaudhry (8)	81
Amandeep Sall (9)	81
Kayleigh Brook (10)	82
Nardeep Manu (11)	82
Elizabeth Olaniyan (11)	83
Nicolle Marshall (10)	83
Anna Rolfe (9)	84
Chianne Bal (10)	84
Samia Chaudhry (10)	84
Eleanor Webb (10)	85
Joseph Lima (9)	85
Freya Penfold (9)	86

Kings Farm Primary School

Jamie Watson (11)	86
Giuseppe Trimarco (11)	87
Luke Todd (11)	87
Michael McGrath (10)	88
Natasha Newstead & Kirsty Morris (11)	88
Megan Osbourne (9)	89
Kirsty Addison (9)	89
Jodie Hamilton (10)	90
Amber Boyle (10)	90
Corrigan Hicks (10)	91
Charlie Pankhurst, Mathew Arney & Michael Newstead (9)	91
McKayla Cullen (9)	91
Craig White (9)	92
George Parker (10)	92

Amy McGrath (9)	93
Jack O'Brien & Jack Parker (10)	93
Amanda Williams (10)	94
Maria Watkins (9)	94
Danny Caller (10)	94
Kirsty Rea (10)	95
Jessica Whyman (10)	95
Naomi Holmes (9)	96
Jemma Frodsham (10)	96
Steven Coleman (10)	97
Jessica Nunnery (10)	97
Joe Loft (9)	98
Joseph Holderness (10)	98
Jemma Evans (10)	99
Natasha Sutton (10)	99
Emma-Louise Coomber (9)	99
Henry Eastwood (10)	100
Emmanuella Torto-Doku (9)	101
Amy Evans (10)	101
Alan Josh (9)	102
Andrew Perry (8)	102
Jade Gibbons (8)	102
Keelley Caller (9)	103
Carly Addison (8)	103
Kieran Harvey (8)	103
Gianluca Trimarco (8)	104
Reece Whyman (9)	104
Marc Hoad (8)	104
Kenny Watkins (10)	105
Jack Andrew (8)	105
Shelby Clare (8)	106
Alexander Williams (9)	106
Jack Howard (8)	106
William Johnson-Cole (8)	107
Taylor Nightingale (8)	107
Emily Davis (8)	107
Charlotte-Marie Garland (9)	108
Ricky Gardner (9)	108

Meopham CP School

Annamarie Tarr (10)	109
Charlotte Clayton (10)	110

Raynehurst Junior School

Lewis Atkinson (9)	110
Paige Martin (10)	111
Elizabeth McDonnell (11)	111
Jade Simpson (9)	112
Robert Bussey (11)	112
Alex Wake (8)	112
Shannon Presland (8)	113
Gemma Holdoway (11)	113
Daniel Jackson (9)	113
James Thomas (9)	114
Jessica Bard (11)	114
Amy Spillett (9)	115
Samuel Davis-Dalton (9)	115
Shanice Faber (10)	116
Kayleigh Tyler (11)	117
Jodie Dixon (10)	117
Kayleigh Hilbert (9)	118
Bobby Akers (9)	118
Jade South (9)	118
Lee Johnson (10)	119
Joshua Armitage (7)	119
Chelsea Swain (7)	119

Riverview Junior School

Maria McCann (9)	120
Emma Bailey (9)	120
Conor Lawlor (8)	121
Jemima Smith (8)	121
Olivia Lawson (8)	122
Sara Port (9)	122
Kevin Richardson (9)	123
Kayleigh Harwood (8)	123
Jed Gamman (8)	124
Hazel Williams (8)	124
Holly Richardson (8)	124

Holly Windsor (9)   125
Naomi Payne (8)   125

St Paulinus CE Primary School, Crayford
Amy Fisher (11)   126
Scott Mitchell & Chris Lees (11)   127
James Mason (10)   128
Leah Jeffery (11)   128
Liam Smith (11)   129
Robert Elliott (11)   130
Callum Togwell (11)   130
Sophie Kingston (10)   131
Jack Phillips (10)   131
Samuel Stone (11)   132
Jack Sharp (11)   133
Max Fountain (10)   134
George Bartholomew (11)   134
Suhanya Jeyashiri (11)   135
Hollie Brown (11)   135
Samantha Selby (10)   136
Jessica Board (11)   136
Lauren Blood (11)   137
Abbie Noakes (10)   137
Alexandra Kerr (11)   138
Holly Board (11)   138
Glen Chute (10)   139
Jasmine Stacey (10)   140

Saxon Way Primary School
Kieron Merritt (11)   140
Lauren Weeks (10)   141
Rhianne Lowe (8)   141
Suann Brignall (11)   142
Abbygail Isitt-Lee (10)   142
Claire Goldsmith (8)   143
Becky Bedwell (11)   143

Sheldwich Primary School
Bethan Evans (9)   144
Emmeline Kerkvliet (11)   144
Emma Godden (9)   145

The Brent Primary School

Shannon Homden (10)	161
Deena Braxton (9)	161
Coy Hardy (10)	162
Ellicia Roberts (9)	162
Harvinder Rai (10)	162
Ryan Cherry (9)	163
Kirstie Weeks (9)	163
Charlotte Wickens (9)	163
Danielle Findlay (10)	164
Kelly Haines (10)	164
Scott Rudd (8)	165
Emma Hannay (9)	165
Leah Shine (10)	166
Oliver Willbye (9)	166
Natasha Nash (9)	167
Charlotte Roffey (10)	167
Rebecca Letchford (9)	167
Abbie Hales (9)	168
Megan Pearson (10)	168
Joseph Reynolds (8)	168
Josh Heaton (9)	169
Daisy Walker (9)	169
Mireille Patrick (9)	169
Joshua Jarvis (9)	170
Emma McCartney (10)	170
Jonathan May (8)	170
Lauren Dixon (11)	171
Danielle McCarthy (11)	171
Emily Thompson (9)	172
Robbie Underhill	172
Luke Newell (8)	173
Marcel Wanstall (8)	173

Twydall Junior School

Krystal Matthews (9)	174
Callum Duce (9)	174
Benjamin Smith (9)	175
Amber Goddard (10)	175
Matthew Hurst (10)	176
Jessica Wood (10)	176
Stelio Furner (10)	177

Jasmine Randall (10)	177
Chantelle Wren (10)	178
Chloe Ponsford (9)	179
Katie Haughton (10)	180
Michael Fegan (10)	180
Jack Stevens (9)	181
Ryan Barrett (10)	181
Joshua Wheddon (10)	182
Alice Tappin (10)	182
James McLuskie (10)	183
Joshua Nicholls (9)	183
David Lownds (10)	184
Molly-Jane Carter (9)	184
Shanice Berko (10)	184
Sophie Aldridge (10)	185
Emma-Lea Millett (9)	185
Ava Darby (9)	186
Scarlett-Jane Mann (9)	186
Katie Stokes (9)	187
Rebecca Coombs (10)	187

Warren Wood Primary School

Jack Mullaney (11)	188
Satveer Kaur (11)	188
Sam Waters (11)	189
Jemma Parsons (10)	189
Rachel Amey-Drew (11)	190
Ryan Stanley (11)	190
Francis Carey (10)	191
Perry Morgan (11)	191
Peter Cole (11)	192
Shayla Sutcliffe (10)	192
Thomas Williams (11)	193
Ashleigh Patrick (10)	193
Jake Shannon (11)	194
Connor Anderson (11)	194
Hannah Burt (10)	195
William Packwood (10)	195
James Tutt (11)	196
Michael Olsen (10)	196

The Poems

The Vicious Waves

The waves were exploding high and low
And were beginning to get worse every minute of the day.
They started lunging at the shore
And didn't bother to go away.

Adults and children came to swim,
For just at least an hour,
The great, massive waves wrecked their backs
And they thought of it as a shower.

They can drive German ships
Into unknown shores
And turned their boats
Into speedboats with oars.

Luke Boucher (11)
Bligh Junior School

Ten Things Found In The Sea

A caring snorkler looking for fish with diseases.
A dolphin calling his mum.
An angry crab snapping trespassers' toes.
A treasure chest full of pirates' gold.
A lonely skeleton in his watery grave.
A shipwreck full of ghostly sailors.
Seaweed swaying in the waves.
Shell full of glittering pearls.
A beautiful mermaid with blonde, flowing hair.
A jellyfish waiting to sting noisy human beings.

Sharlie Jarvis (11)
Bligh Junior School

The Angry Sea

Waves crash and bash up the cliffside,
Like a mountain climber
Falling to meet the roaring sea
And its mighty attacks.
And when he falls,
The tidal wave swallowing him,
Like a surfer beginning to get away from it quickly.

Connor Smith (11)
Bligh Junior School

Ten Things Found In The Sea

A caring snorkler looking for fish with diseases.
A dolphin calling his mum.
An angry crab snapping trespassers' toes.
A treasure chest full of pirates' gold.
A lonely skeleton in his watery grave.
A shipwreck full of ghostly sailors.
Seaweed swaying in the waves.
A shell full of glittering pearls.
A beautiful mermaid with blonde, flowing hair.
A jellyfish waiting to sting noisy human beings.

Demi Rossiter
Bligh Junior School

Would You?

How would you like to see
The mountain's snowy peak
And the howling of your echoes die?
Not I!

How would you like to hear
A dog's beautiful bark
And the cry of a dog disappear?
Not me!

David Field (10)
Bligh Junior School

Waves

I collide with ships on purpose,
Without a care in the world.
I drive onto beaches,
Hoping to get up the rocks.
I drown anyone who swims in me,
With my monstrous waves as big as Everest.

I can wreck ships made of wood,
Or submarines if I could.
I suck people into my whirlpools,
Then flood the nearest schools.
I can create deadly waves, that I can be,
Or dash around the sea, which is me.

I can sink what I like
And play with fish like pike.
I can flood mighty towns,
Or watch icebergs fall down.
I can grab falling treasure with my hand
And keep it forever in a box made of sand.
When I am devastated, I shout and scream,
But when I am tranquil, I relax and eat ice cream.

Zoe Hosking (11)
Bligh Junior School

Would You?

How would you like to see . . .
The world in black and white with . . .
No freedom
No happiness
No light?

How would you like not to hear . . .
Birds fluttering about
No dogs barking at the cats above
No hissing from the cats
No sound from the howling whales?

Cassie Griffin (11)
Bligh Junior School

The Claws Of The Sea

I am the waves, the claws of the sea,
I try to cause destruction to anything I see.

I can bash and smother boats whole,
I can pull the mightiest people down to my dingy depths,
Then I take their life to be mine.

I can destroy the greatest cliffs of all time,
I soar up high and crash down low,
Smashing and dashing anything I meet.

Then I unleash my foamy white horses
Which charge up the beach, but eventually retreat,
Dragging their prey back to me.

Now this is when I get really annoyed,
I destroy anything I can see or that dares to come near me,
This is why everyone must fear me.

James Ozanne (10)
Bligh Junior School

The Fierce And Violent Wave!

I am the wave.
I am the fierce and violent wave.

I can make boats bob up and down
And make people go bright red,

And then when it's time for bed,
I just have more fun, fun, fun,

'Cause I am the fierce and violent wave,
Nobody wants to swim in me,

Because I am the fierce and violent wave,
The fierce and violent wave.

Cassie Hill (10)
Bligh Junior School

The Destructive Sea

I crush boats with my strong fingertips,
Take ships down into my whirlpool that never escape.

Chuck fishing boats into the rough rocks,
Rip things apart and drag them down to my dirty den.

Sea creatures try to scarper away, but can't,
I spit at people when they walk on the shore.

I can do terrible things, terrible, terrible things,
I creep up on anything that gets in my way with my powerful,
destructive waves.

I am the terrible, vicious sea,
I pounce on my victims like a tiger.

I roar like a lion,
I take down prey like a rhino.

Then I die down finally, finally, finally.

Jamie Lancaster (11)
Bligh Junior School

Would You?

How would you like to see,
No animals left
For you and me?
Not me!

How would you like to see,
No waterfalls falling down
Or whooshing around?
Definitely not me!

Chloe Dance (11)
Bligh Junior School

The Invincible Wave

I am a violent wave,
I'm as tall as a tower,
No one can stop me,
When I have my power.

I am a lion,
My body curling like Quavers,
I have no fear of anything,
When I look down upon the bathers.

When I crash into ships
And make adults go mad,
My fishes cry, my sharks die
And then I am bad.

I weigh 20 tonnes,
That crash to the ground,
The people watch
And then they drown.

I turn very violent,
And everyone runs,
I get so mad,
That dads grab their sons.

Jake Tubby (10)
Bligh Junior School

The Blue Waves

I'm the white horse who rides the sea at night.
I'm violent and vicious, *beware!*
Be careful because I can give you a fright.
I come every five minutes, come in if you dare!
I will put you in my whirlpool.
I can just smash you into pieces.
I'm just like a dangerous tool,
So no one had better come near, *or else!*

Lucy-Ann Morris (11)
Bligh Junior School

Would You?

How would you like to see
Open spaces disappear
And never be seen again
Built on with houses and buildings?
Not me!

How would you like to hear
The sound of a saw
Cutting down the forest
And wild animals running away?
Not I!

Tansy Hammond (10)
Bligh Junior School

River, River

River, river why don't you talk?
River, river talk to me!
River, river where do you go?
River, river do you go to the sea?

Liam Fagg (8)
Bligh Junior School

Waves

Round like curly, crunchy Quavers,
Like sharks pushing hard against your feet
With the force of a rhino pushing down a tree,
Twisting and twirling like a hurricane wind.
The weight of an elephant sitting on you,
The sound of loud, thumping music,
The strength of a bull trying to get to shore,
A galloping horse charging towards you.
With the smell of a salty fish market,
The twist of a roller coaster that brings you down.

Kelly Roots (10)
Bligh Junior School

The Powerful Waves

The waves are as big as a building
And they smash a load of things.

They splash upon the base of the pier,
The people now have a huge fear.

The sea makes a thunder,
Then drags people under.

The waves are like horses jumping,
Then they go back under with their hearts thumping.

The sparkling fishes whirling through the waves,
Then they get tired and go in their caves.

Lauren Solly (10)
Bligh Junior School

The Powerful Sea

I, the sea, am the great provider,
I give everyone the sea and water.

I am the almighty sea,
Nothing at all is better than me.

I was as graceful as a ballerina,
Until everyone started to swim.

That big iceberg is making me cold,
But I am still big and bold.

I make the great giant waves,
It hurts when I crash against the caves.

Amy Tolladay (11)
Bligh Junior School

The Violent Waves

The waves are as big as a house,
Which make sharks as small as a mouse.

The wave weighs more than iron,
They are violent like a hungry lion.

Waves flood fleets of ships
And squeeze through people's lips.

The waves are like horses jumping,
Which make people's hearts start thumping.

They do grab boats in their sight
And take them for a gentle flight.

Now they are calm like a sleeping baby
And suddenly jump up. Would they? Maybe.

Helen Richards (11)
Bligh Junior School

The Australian Waves

Waves colliding against a rock,
Making lots of bubbly froth.
Curling, whirling round the sea,
Playing in it, you and me.
Not having much fun,
Not realising how they come and come.
Waves jumping up and down,
Then going round and round.
Surfing through the waves,
Call it playing games.
Waves come to a stop
And are hiding behind a rock.

Hannah Stead (11)
Bligh Junior School

The Waves

I am curly like Quavers,
I roar, riot and shout,
Am taller than a tower.

I show my power,
I'm a dangerous sea,
I go high, then low.

Am larger than an elephant,
People come to visit me,
But as I make my waves,
They leave and return another day.

I crash and bash, am deadly,
That's what people say.
I tumble and jump just to get to shore.
I take my last breath as I make my last roar.

Tracy Craig (10)
Bligh Junior School

Waves

Round and curly like crunchy Quavers,
Like sharks pushing hard at your feet,
With the force of a rhino pushing down a tree,
Twisting and twirling like a hurricane wind,
The weight of an elephant sitting on you,
The sound of loud, thumping music,
The strength of a bull trying to get to shore,
A galloping horse charging towards you,
With the smell of a salty fish market,
The twist of a roller coaster that brings you down.

Jamie Russell (11)
Bligh Junior School

Destructive Waves

The waves are like galloping, furious horses,
They emerge whenever and wherever they like,
They curl like the giant hand of a tiger,
When they fall on you, they feel like a huge, sharp, cold spike.

On stormy days, waves shriek and roar,
Make terrible shipwrecks,
Crack the wooden planks on ships
And drown all people on deck.

Soon waves calm and people are pleased,
They bathe in the sand,
Go to the parks
And some boats arrive back on the land.

Ashleigh Lewis (11)
Bligh Junior School

The Monstrous Waves

I will be strong, never mild,
I'm never calm, always wild.

I curl like paws of a tiger,
Can I be any wilder?

Of course I can, I'll drown my victims,
I'll land on them like one hundred tonnes,
Mums, dads and their sons.

But tomorrow, I will be calm,
For now I'll slay you with my might,
So run, run out of sight.

Joseph Dodson (11)
Bligh Junior School

The Angry Waves!

I can curl up like a Quaver with a salty flavour,
I come crashing down like a tiger pouncing and bouncing.

I make the weight that will kill a person and their mate,
If there's a boat I will swallow it in spite.

Sometimes I make a wave so that no one can be saved,
People are screaming and hoping they are dreaming.

Michael Brenchley (10)
Bligh Junior School

Sweeping

You are sweeping
Through the waves of life,
Twisting and turning,
This way and that.
You are sweeping
Into a deep, dark, wonderful world.
We are one.
The whole, wide, wonderful world.

Alison Byrne (8)
Bligh Junior School

Eight Things Found In The Sea

A caring snorkler looking for fish with diseases
A dolphin calling his mum
An angry crab snapping at trespassers' toes
A treasure chest full of pirates' gold
A lonely skeleton in his watery grave
A ship full of ghostly sailors
Seaweed swaying in the waves
A shell full of clattering pearls.

Georgina Satchell (10)
Bligh Junior School

Would You?

Would you like to see
Oceans and seas
Dried up
So people can't live?
      Not me!

Would you like to see
All the trees in the world
Cut down
So there wouldn't be any shade?
      Not I!

Chelsea Malcolm (11)
Bligh Junior School

What Is Blue?

Blue is the sky
Where bluebirds fly.
Blue is a sparkling gem
In the centre of the Queen's crown.
Blue is the sea
On a toy key.
Blue is a silky material
On an Indian's dress.
Blue is the water
Bubbling in a rock pool.
Blue is a bluebell
Swaying in the breeze.
Blue is the rain
Drumming on the windowpane.
Blue is a colour of the rainbow
When the rain falls.

Sophie Cherry (8)
Bredhurst CE Primary School

What Is Yellow?

Yellow is a flower
Swaying in the breeze.
Yellow is twinkling stars
Dancing in the sky.
Yellow is a lemon
Squeezed on pancakes.
Yellow is the hot, shiny sun
Shining on the shimmering sea.
Yellow is golden sand
Tickling our feet.
Yellow is a squashy marshmallow
Eaten all up by us.
Yellow is a flickering fire flame
Dancing on Bonfire Night.
Yellow is yummy ice cream
Melting on a hot summer's day.
Yellow is a fish showing off its scales
In the blue ocean.
Yellow are old autumn leaves
Lying on the mossy grass.

Ellis Holland (7)
Bredhurst CE Primary School

What Is Green?

Green is a grassy field where the white sheep play.
Green is a slippery, shiny fish swimming and jumping in the
                                                blue ocean.
Green is a tree where the fluttering birds play and sing.
Green is a racing car speeding round a racing track.
Green is a pen writing away at Bredhurst CE Primary School.

Freeman Rogers (8)
Bredhurst CE Primary School

What Is Red?

Red is a love heart
To send on Valentine's Day.
Red is a fox
Strolling in the dusk for food.
Red is a zooming Ferrari
Zooming around the bendy track.
Red is a shiny apple
On a big, beautiful apple tree.
Red is a sparkling jelly
Wobbling on a big round plate.
Red is a shiny car
Zooming on the M2.
Red is boiling lava
In a rocky volcano.
Red is a shiny balloon
Floating in the bright blue sky.

James Macdonald (8)
Bredhurst CE Primary School

What Is Blue?

Blue is the summer sky
On the hot, sandy beach.
Blue is the shiny water
Running down the drains.
Blue is the salty sea
Sparkling in the ocean.
Blue is the sticky glue
Sticking bows on a birthday card.
Blue is the bath water
Coming up to the middle of my body.

Gemma Sweetman (7)
Bredhurst CE Primary School

What Is Red?

Red is a love heart
To send on Valentine's Day.
Red is a Ferrari
Blasting round the track.
Vans are red
With blood on them.
Red is a bruise
Shining on your finger.
Red is jelly
Wobbling on a plate.
Red is a shiny apple
On a big, beautiful apple tree.
Red is glass
Sparkling on the table.

Liam Choak (7)
Bredhurst CE Primary School

What Is Blue?

Blue is the summer sky
On the hot, sandy beach.

Blue is the shiny water
Running down the drains.

Blue is the salty sea
Sparkling in the ocean.

Blue is the sticky glue
Being used to make a Christmas card.

Blue is the bath
Bubbling up to your middle.

Sophie Bennett (7)
Bredhurst CE Primary School

What Is Blue?

Blue is a shiny sky
Shining on the bluebells up high.
Blue is a windy mist
Whistling on the shore.
Blue is a computer trolley
It is not better than a bubblegum lolly.
Blue is an envelope
Shimmering in the postbox.
Blue is an enormous whale
Diving in the calm sea.
Blue is a rock pool
Swaying in the breeze.
Blue is a barbecue
Sizzling in the sun.
Blue is an eyepatch
Covering an evil eye.
Blue is a cape
Swaying over a blueberry pie!

Grace Walton (8)
Bredhurst CE Primary School

What Is Blue?

Blue is the water
Pouring down a waterfall.
Blue is a bluebell
Swaying in the breeze.
Blue is the rain
Drumming on the windowpane.
Blue is a colour in the rainbow
When the rain falls.

Georgia Wilkinson (7)
Bredhurst CE Primary School

What Is Yellow?

Yellow is a flower
Singing in the breeze.
Yellow is a twinkly star
Dancing in the trees.
Yellow is a juicy lemon
Squeezed on pancakes.
Yellow is a hot sun
Shining down on us.
Yellow is a flickering fire flame
Dancing on Bonfire Night.
Yellow is a fish
Showing off its glittery scales in the ocean.
Yellow is golden sand
Tickling our feet.
Yellow is a squashy marshmallow
Eaten up by us.
Yellow is a yummy ice cream
Melting on a hot summer's day.

Bethany Fleming (8)
Bredhurst CE Primary School

Red

Red is a love heart
To send on Valentine's Day.
Red is a blood-red fox
Running in the forest.
Red is a zooming Ferrari
And it is zooming around the track.
Red is boiling hot lava
Sliding down the volcano.
Red is a jelly
Wriggling on a china plate.

Jessica Sheehan (7)
Bredhurst CE Primary School

What Is Blue?

Blue is an enormous blue whale
Diving in the ocean.
Blue is a rock pool
Swishing in the breeze.
Blue is a barbecue
Sizzling in the sun.
Blue is a water pistol
Squirting in the hotness.
Blue is a rubbish bin
Sitting in the street.
Blue is a beetle
Creeping in the grass.
Blue is an eye patch
Covering up an evil eye.

James Adamson (7)
Bredhurst CE Primary School

What Is Red?

Red is lava
Rumbling around in a volcano.
Red is a ball
In the World Cup final.
Red is a boiling oven
In the kitchen.
Red is a nice juicy apple
On an apple tree.
Red is a strawberry
In a flower bed.

Joshua Hannan (7)
Bredhurst CE Primary School

What Is Red?

Red is a red, red rose on the Queen's shiny, sparkly crown
Red is the top of Cupid's arrow
Red is the scab on my leg
Red is a literacy book
Red is lava.

Thomas Barton (8)
Bredhurst CE Primary School

What I Like

I like pizza
I like chips
I like custard
And chocolate dips

I like silver
I like blue
I like gold
And black too

I like maths
I like PE
I like English
And RE

I like tennis
I like football
I like cricket
And basketball

I like oranges
I like cherries
I like peaches
And berries.

Mamunur Rahman (9)
Chantry Primary School

Flowers

My favourite flowers are roses.

R is for red
   which roses can be
   like a fiery sunset
   which burns within me.

O is for odour
   the beautiful smell of a rose
   so light, so sweet
   I could smell it from dusk till dawn.

S is for silk
   delicate as can be
   spun from a petal
   especially made for you and me.

E is for elegant
   as it stands tall
   with its beautiful and graceful movements
   as the wind blows
   softly across the fields.

S is for simplistic but sophistication
   a flower that is truly
   filled with imagination.

Sadia Khalid (10)
Chantry Primary School

Snow

S now blows like a piece of dough
N ever let it go
O ver the hill and far away
W ill it snow today?

Holly Marchant (9)
Chantry Primary School

Football

Football is the best,
Better than the rest,
Played in the west,
So put it to the test.

It may look rough,
So you have to be tough,
You can dodge them with some skill,
To keep the score two-nil.

When you kick the ball,
Make sure not to fall,
Aim for the goal,
But not the pole.

I'm a big fan,
Who's glad it's not banned,
It's a big theme,
To watch my great team.

The cup they bring home with pride,
Ensure not to hide,
But show it to all,
Because of the great ball.

Suleman Hussain (10)
Chantry Primary School

My Fairy Godmother

My fairy godmother likes to sing
My fairy godmother has a habit of flapping her left wing
She likes to spin and toss around
But sometimes she falls to the ground.

She likes to think about things to eat
Even when she's off her feet
After a long and tiring day
She goes up in the sky and flutters away.

Jade Sargun (9)
Chantry Primary School

Netball

Netball is rough
Netball is tough
Don't play on grass
You might trip over and pass
You play as a team
And shoot as steam
Try to jump tall
So you can catch the ball
Try not to play in the cold
Our uniforms are bright and bold
Try hard to score a goal
But don't hit it on the pole
Don't throw the ball over the court
You might get caught
Now it's time to go
Don't be sad if you didn't win
But next time you will win
And fall in a bin.

Natasha Khalid (9)
Chantry Primary School

All About Love

The love I give to family
The joy I give to friends
It shows that I appreciate
The love that never ends

And when there's no one left
It builds up in your heart
But your family's still with you
And you will never be apart.

Charlie Webb (9)
Chantry Primary School

All About Boys

Boys are lazy
Boys are crazy

They always fight
And wake up in the night

They are bad
And never sad

They throw things that are rotten
And chuck things that are cotton

They carry a bag
And play 'tag'

They run around
And fall on the ground

They are the best
In the west.

Zubair Ashraf (8)
Chantry Primary School

Don't Do That

Don't do that.
Don't do that.
Don't kick the cat
And don't smack the bat.
Don't do anything more like that.
Don't say that.
Don't draw the bat
And don't draw anymore like that.
Save some for the poor like that,
Don't say anyone is fat like that
And don't stick the cat next to the bat
Like that.
Now you don't have anything more like that.

Sunil Sidhu (9)
Chantry Primary School

Dogs

Dogs are fun, furry and cuddly.
They have long hair and short hair.
Some have no hair, dogs are fun.
I like dogs best, they are better than the rest.

You can play with them, you can walk with them
And you can sit with them.
Dogs love us, so we should love them.
Look after them, care for them.
They are loyal to us, as we are to them.

Dogs have long tails, dogs have short tails.
They all wag when they are happy.
When they play, when they run.

Dogs love to chase, they love to swim.
They have to wash, they love to chew.
They love toys, with which they play.
They can go on and on all day.

Emma Alvis (9)
Chantry Primary School

Cousin Neville

Speak of the Devil
Meet cousin Neville

If he is in bed
He must be dead

If he is awake
He will slash you with a rake

Speak of Neville
Meet the Devil

Now you know the true story of Neville
Don't blame me, blame the Devil.

Klajdi Alikaj (9)
Chantry Primary School

My Favourite Lesson

My favourite lesson is PE
It would have to be.
My teacher's name is Miss Hosty
But she can be quite bossy.

We played in the pool
We used lots of balls.
I had my hair in a bun
And the lesson was quite fun.

We had quite a lot of free time
It was lunchtime.
The button was pressed
So it was time to get dressed.

Charanjit Kaur Samra (10)
Chantry Primary School

My Hamster

My hamster, Molly
Is always bright and jolly,
She likes to eat all sorts of food,
Apple, banana, nuts and bread,
She stores them in her pouches
To carry to her bed.

Her fur is fluffy and eyes so bright,
She always comes out when it is night.
She climbs up her cage using the bars,
She does it so easy, she must be a star.

She is so small and quick,
Never takes a rest,
It's easy to say,
My hamster's the best.

Jack Boyd (10)
Chantry Primary School

All About Football

Football, football is like a dream,
I think of football when I'm asleep.

It's so wonderful to play football,
I dream of winning the World Cup for England.

When I play football,
I huff and puff and also my team can get a little rough.

Football is fun,
We always run.

We have a rest,
But also we are the best.

We always play football on Mondays,
But the best is played on Wednesdays,
So we don't bother on Sundays.

When I run with the ball under the sun,
I really have a lot of fun.

When I am running after the ball,
I sometimes get in a tackle and trip and fall.

Junaid Khalid (9)
Chantry Primary School

Love

The love for my family
The love for my friends
I thought it was hard, I thought again
The love for my friends
Is different than I thought
The love for my family means a lot
The love for my friends
The love for my family
It is always here, it will never end.

Jaid Stevens (10)
Chantry Primary School

Lion Dreams

When I go to bed at night
And my mum's turned off the light
I close my eyes and in my head
I'm in Africa, not in bed.

Underneath a light blue sky
I see a lion running by
In her mouth she holds her prey
Enough to last her for the day.

I follow her and then I see
Three tiny cubs looking at me
Lovely little bundles of fun
Playing in the blazing sun.

Mum is tearing at the meat
Then suddenly she's on her feet
Staring at me with an angry face
Running towards me at a deadly pace.

I heard the thumping of her paws
And wished that I was safe indoors
The lion's eyes had a wicked gleam
I'm so glad it was just a dream!

Lisa Gardiner (10)
Chantry Primary School

Back To School

I got up in a hurry
I went in a scurry
My room was in a mess
I even wore a dress
When I got to school
I looked just like a fool
The children had a laugh
Along with all the staff.

Robeni Ali (10)
Chantry Primary School

All About My Parents

My mum's the best
Better than all the rest

She gives me a hug
When I have a bug

Cos when I'm ill
She gives me a pill

She looks after us
Even on a bus

She gives us a sweet
As a treat

When we play
On a hot summer's day

My dad buys a fan
And brings it in the van

Even if it's hot
We still have to drink a lot

At night we look at the sky
Which is very, very high

We'll see the moon
Very, very soon

We count stars
Which are up above near Mars

So when it's time for bed
I accidentally bump my head

And I have a bump
With a great big lump

So when I'm sad
All I have to do is run to my dad

So he gives me a cuddle
When I'm in a muddle.

Zoheb Ashraf (9)
Chantry Primary School

Jelly

I was eating jelly and it started to wobble
In my belly while I was watching telly,
I burped
And it was very smelly.

Mum walked in and gave me a grin,
And said, 'That's not very nice.'
To my surprise I burped again,
My mum said, 'That was twice.'

I did not burp again that night,
My burps were not a very nice sight.
But eating jelly,
Makes you smelly,
I can't help it, they just come,
But I did promise my mum.

Emma Fitchett (9)
Chantry Primary School

Flowers

Flowers are red
Flowers are blue
Flowers are pretty, just like you
I like flowers that are pink
They give a lovely stink
Flowers are wonderful in every way
I don't know what to say
Flowers are yellow
Flowers are green
Even when you turn sixteen
Flowers are planted in the ground
Oh look, I found something round!

Nisha Chowdury (10)
Chantry Primary School

Dr X

(Sung to the tune of Jingle Bells)

Dr X, Dr X
Evil all the way
Oh what fun it is to crush
The world with my death-ray
Hey
Dr X, Dr X
Evil all the way
When you die
I will cry and I will say
Ha, ha, ha
Ha, ha, ha
Ha, ha, ha
Ha, ha, ha
Dr X's crushing today.

Elliott Granger (9)
Chantry Primary School

Number Poem

One, two, Scooby-Doo!
Three, four, open the door.
Five, six, break some sticks.
Seven, eight, I need a new mate.
Nine, ten, crash Big Ben.
Eleven, twelve, naughty elves.
Thirteen, fourteen, I hate gluten.
Fifteen, sixteen, I like remixing.
Seventeen, eighteen, what are you making?
Nineteen, twenty, sleep gently.

Navjeet Singhsall (9)
Chantry Primary School

A Cow That Is Trapped In A Well

We start off with a cow,
That is trapped somehow,
She's trapped in a well,
As far as we can tell,
She can't get out,
Might be a gout,
Or it could just be,
Though it's hard to see,
She wanted to take a bath,
Or just have a swim for a laugh.

Stacey Williams (10)
Chantry Primary School

Once Upon A Rhyme

One day in the town of Legion,
In the land of Once Upon a Rhyme,
There was a food fight between the aliens of Pluto
And the mutant fish of Lustra Dyme.

There were ice fingers flying in people's faces
And custard pies everywhere,
And also no hiding places,
Sprite was in people's hair.

And there was even more chaos
When the aliens set a bear loose
And the mutant fish fired a weapon -
A furious, speeding goose.

The town was in a mess,
There wasn't a single clean dress.
A very important person was visiting the town
In her best dressing gown.

What would the Queen say about this place?
Probably,
 'What a disgrace!'

Jack Fryer (10)
Cliffe Woods Primary School

Once Upon A Rhyme

Football, football,
What a game,
It's one cool sport,
Kick-off again!

Sliding tackles,
What a gamble,
Two-footed challenges,
Not too great.

Yellow cards,
What a shame,
Red cards,
Not again.

Shooting high,
Shooting low,
Oh no,
They've scored a goal!

James Lewis (11)
Cliffe Woods Primary School

I Went To The Zoo

I went to the zoo
I thought it was great.
My mum's at home
Baking a cake.
I saw a giraffe
And it started to laugh.
The hippo decided
To have a mud bath.
I saw a monkey
It looked quite funky.
I saw a lion
It started to run.
My day at the zoo
Was great fun.

Alisa Hanger (10)
Cliffe Woods Primary School

Once Upon A Rhyme

The sun was glowing brightly
My shorts were done up tightly
My boots were clean and shiny
The crowds sounded whiney
The ref blew the whistle loud
I booted the ball into the crowd
I ran, I dodged, I hit the pole
It nearly was a terrific goal
Now the goalie was about to kick
Who the heck's he gonna pick?
Waiting anxiously for the ball
The boy behind had a nasty fall
I helped him up and brushed him down
He played footie like a clown
I got the ball and ran so fast
I scored a goal, oh what a blast!
We won the trophy and held it high
All our team started to cry!

Lewis Cook (10)
Cliffe Woods Primary School

What Am I? Kennings

An ear deafener
A party decorator
A rubber popper
A bang frightener
A gob smacker
A pin popper.
A loud banger
A bang boomer
A party popper
A skin jumper.

Jessica Reuter (9)
Cliffe Woods Primary School

Once Upon A Rhyme

Once upon a rhyme,
When I first had a dream,
It was a very weird time,
When nothing could be seen.

I searched all around,
First high, then low,
Until I heard a sound,
From beneath me in the snow.

I shrieked, 'Oh no,
What is that sound?'
So I said, 'So?'
Because nothing was found.

Suddenly I heard the sound again,
So I ran, ran and ran,
I must be insane,
Since I found it was my nan holding a pan!

Natasha Tyson (10)
Cliffe Woods Primary School

The Scream

Fear is a shadowy figure
Looming over me at night.
Icy fingers creep towards me
Madness stares at me.
Spooky thoughts roam in my mind
Mysterious voices terrify my brain.
Weird and terrifying, ghastly thoughts
Invade my brain as I think.
A strong wind shivers down my back
I stopped and thought and then I heard a scream.
My sweat trickled down my face
A freaky sound swam round my bedroom.
My brain concussed with nightmares
And they are still around my bedroom.

Rochelle Leslie (10)
Cliffe Woods Primary School

Once Upon A Rhyme

Once upon a rhyme, in the fairytale time,
Lived a cat and a mouse, in an old wonky house.

Once upon a rhyme, when the cat turned nine,
The mouse was still eight, when he ran under the gate.

Once upon a rhyme, in a fairytale time,
The mouse fell into a pond and met a fish called James Bond.

The fish said to the mouse, 'Take me to your house.'
The mouse heard the magic talking fish
And hoped he might be granted a cool, big wish.

So the mouse brought the fish back,
Carrying him in his small rucksack.
He put the fish into a safe little den
And then he looked around for another fishy friend.

The cat came down the stairs that day,
To have a good time and a bit of a play.
Also, he wanted to fly his kite,
But not before he saw the fish had a good meal that night!

Elise Pocock (10)
Cliffe Woods Primary School

What Am I?

A loud banger
A kid frightener
A dog frightener
A bright shiner
A cylinder spinner
A fast flyer
A baby crier
A colour maker
What am I?

(A firework)

Daniel Kiernan (9)
Cliffe Woods Primary School

Once Upon A Rhyme

Once upon a rhyme,
Somewhere in time,
There lived a medieval race.

They owned swords and shields,
Acres of fields,
Their numbers exceedingly high,
They sat down to dine,
With goblets of wine,
Which came from a country afar.

There once was a terrible battle,
Between dark and light,
But fortunately good prevailed.

Now I've told my story,
About the warriors' glory,
I shall end this tale,
That happened once upon a rhyme.

Christopher Bateman (11)
Cliffe Woods Primary School

Scream

Fear is a shadowy figure,
Looming over me at night.
Icy fingers creep towards me,
Madness stares at me.
Freaky faces screaming at me,
Creeping stairs slowly.
Murderous figures crawling quickly,
Night is ghostly.
Night is going but the bloodthirsty creature
Is still and it is hungry.
My head is thundering like Hell.

Andrew Rockett (10)
Cliffe Woods Primary School

Once Upon A Rhyme

Once upon a sporty rhyme,
I went for a *gigantic* climb.
Up the great Mount Snowdon,
Where I took my mature son.
Then we went white water rafting,
And me and my son started to sing.
Next we rowed across the River Thames,
And me and my son cleaned the camera lens,
To take a picture of the incredible sun,
As usually it never comes!
Then me and my son went skiing,
We hit a rock with a big *ping!*
Next I taught my son how to fly a plane,
But when I gave him the controls he went insane!
After that I had *a lot* of injuries,
So I decided not to give my son the car keys.
Perhaps I should wait until my son's older than *three!*
I might even wait until he's *as old as me!*

Michael Connolly (11)
Cliffe Woods Primary School

What Am I? Kennings

A high screamer
A loud giggler
A naughty stealer
A food hunter
A baby jumper
A big leaper
An amazing twirler
A food eater
A gum smacker
A tree swinger
What am I?

(A ?????)

Leighton Wynn (9)
Cliffe Woods Primary School

Once Upon A Rhyme

Once upon a disastrous rhyme,
My evil half-brother committed a serious crime.
He robbed our neighbour and broke the door,
He ended up on a cell floor!

Once upon a careless rhyme,
My so-called angel sister lost track of time.
She burnt the dinner and smashed a glass,
She let next-door's dog foul on our grass!

Once upon an emotional rhyme,
My poor old mother only drank lemon and lime.
The reason for that was Trebor died,
He tried to fly but . . . Mum cried and cried.
Now she's over him, she buys velour,
To remind her of Trebor's fur!

Once upon a joyful rhyme,
My family are here peeling, like bells that chime.
We are all happy, happy we are,
My brother has a job and Mum has a new car!

This is my once upon a rhyme!

Leah Johnson (11)
Cliffe Woods Primary School

The Scream

Fear is a shadowy giant
Looming over me at night
Icy fingers creep towards me
Madness stares at me
Its freaky mouth snapping open and shut
The scream screeching in my ears
Its eyes murderously moving around
The ghastly creature hovers near me
The creepy nightmare locked to my brain
The tormented atmosphere goes shockingly mad
The sinister monster now ready for the kill!

Daniel Gilbert (10)
Cliffe Woods Primary School

Once Upon A Rhyme

Once upon a magical rhyme,
I found myself in the medieval time.
I asked someone, 'Where am I?'
They replied, '1549.'

I ran around going mad,
I really thought this was bad.
Then a princess came up to me,
She said that her name was Leigh.

I said, 'I need to go home now!'
She said she would help with her spotted cow!
We searched around for hours on end,
But then we turned the right bend.

We had found the right way back,
I didn't really need to pack.
I ran off shouting, 'Thank you!'
This experience was brand new.

Alice Penney (10)
Cliffe Woods Primary School

What Am I? Kennings

I'm a bottle holder
A page turner
A pen grabber
A back scratcher
A hand holder
A head scratcher
An ear cleaner
A sign maker
An eye plucker
A hard worker
A rib tickler
A personal fan.

What am I?
(A hand)

Rosanne Seath (11)
Cliffe Woods Primary School

What Am I? Kennings

A great season
A good reason
A tree fairy
A holy Mary
A roast dinner
A stocking opener
A happy child
A sweet heaven
A relation rounder
A cracker buyer
A big fire
A young desire
A church day.
What am I?

(Christmas)

Laura Monahan (10)
Cliffe Woods Primary School

Once Upon A Rhyme

Arsenal with the ball
There's no time to stall
As the goal is calling
For a second time

There they go with such great skill
Are they going to shoot?
Of course they will
Goal!

Arsene Wenger in such great cheer
Now he knows they're two points clear

The fans go wild
While the others are mild
They're all in shock
They've got jaw lock.

Jordan Bannon (10)
Cliffe Woods Primary School

Once Upon A Rhyme

This is my rhyme
And I'll take you back in time,
To the cruel creature,
To the moaning teacher.
I was at the school door
And I wasn't sure.
I looked around with a mysterious glare,
Oh no! Here he comes down the stairs.
It's the teacher from hell!
At the moment I was not swell.
He pulled me through and in,
And my shirt was burning my skin.
He dragged me right past,
Where the children were last.
They jumped out the way,
Not knowing what to say.
I tried and tried to tug away,
But I was late so I had to stay.
He kept me in throughout break,
That should teach me what time I wake.

Kristian Mantalvanos (11)
Cliffe Woods Primary School

What Am I? Kennings

A grey plodder
A fat noser
A noisy eater
A hairy monster
A short tail swinger
A slow mover
A scaredy-cat
A tree wrecker
A corrugated noser
An eyelash blinker.
What am I?

Fabia Gould (10)
Cliffe Woods Primary School

Once Upon A Rhyme

I live in a road called Once Upon A Rhyme,
We all speak in rhyme.
We sing our songs in rhyme,
I live in a road called Once Upon A Rhyme.

I live in a road called Once Upon A Rhyme,
We sleep in rhyme,
We wake up in rhyme,
We eat our breakfast in rhyme,
We walk in rhyme,
We go to school in rhyme,
We do our work in rhyme,
We eat our lunch in rhyme,
We go home in rhyme,
We play in rhyme,
I live in a road called Once Upon A Rhyme.

I live in a road called Once Upon A Rhyme,
I really like my road where we talk in rhyme,
I really like my road where we sleep in rhyme,
I live in a road called Once Upon A Rhyme.

Charlotte Frampton (10)
Cliffe Woods Primary School

The Scream

Fear is a shadowy figure
Looming over me at night!
Icy fingers creep towards me!
Madness stares at me!
Murderous screams ring in my ears!
The creepy atmosphere circles in the gloomy night!
My brain suffering with horror!
The tormenting smell of Hell in my nose!
My spine clicks at every move I make!
The mysterious scream, of the Devil from Hell!

Matthew Leng (10)
Cliffe Woods Primary School

Once Upon A Rhyme

Once upon a rhyme,
There was a time,
Where people lived in huts,
And those people ate nuts
And the nearby mine
Would dig up dimes.

But in outer space,
There was a place,
Where creatures lived at home,
Inside a dome.

Back on Earth,
There was turf,
Where no man dared go,
Because of the Low,
A spirit that swept across the land,
Turning good into bad.

And the rich,
Would live in a ditch,
But the poor,
Would live indoors.
So what sort of place was this?
It was called the land of Zish.

Lee Wallis (11)
Cliffe Woods Primary School

What Am I? Kennings

A whizz banger,
A sky splitter,
A silence breaker,
A sky lighter,
A shape spinner,
An air exploder,
A bang crackler,
A whistle cracker,
A no kid fiddler,
A cat scarer,
A heart jumper,
An exciting exploder,
A sky soarer,
A high banger,
A fierce burner,
A finger eater,
A flying exciter,
A gunpowder blower,
A sizzling shiner,
A light entertainer,
A dog frightener.
What am I?

(A firework)

Samuel Moore (10)
Cliffe Woods Primary School

What Am I? Kennings

I'm a head banger
I'm a back slapper
I'm a bottle holder
I'm a happy waver
I'm a hard worker
I'm a lip painter
I'm a rib tickler
I'm a page turner
I'm a book handler
I'm a hand holder
I'm a face cooler
I'm a sign maker
I'm an ear cleaner
I'm an eyelash plucker
I'm a happy worker
I'm an eye cleaner.

What am I?
(A hand)

Charlotte Dyett-Hughes (10)
Cliffe Woods Primary School

What Am I?

A grass burner
A sky lighter
An ear popper
An orbit maker
A bang maker
A high flyer
A whizzing flame
A tube of fun.
What am I?

(A firework)

Ryan Hastings (11)
Cliffe Woods Primary School

What Is It? Kennings

An air shaker,
A big danger,
An eardrum blower,
A people killer,
A hair raiser,
A ground opener,
A house shaker,
A fire maker,
A people hater,
A ground shaker,
A gas maker,
An animal killer,
A ship sinker,
A cloud mover,
A poison maker,
A spark maker,
A bone shaker,
A nuclear danger,
A noise maker,
A hell maker.

What is it?
(A bomb)

Ashley Belsey (10)
Cliffe Woods Primary School

The Scream!

Fear is a shadowy figure
Looming over me at night
Icy fingers creep towards me
Madness stares at me
Mysterious thoughts scream in my tormented head
Death detached to my breaking bones.

Zoë Aggett (11)
Cliffe Woods Primary School

What Am I? Kennings

A fast spinner,
A bad burner,
A spark flyer,
A colour changer,
A dog frightener,
A fence changer,
A night shiner,
A rocket speeder,
A mad flyer,
A fence burner,
A plant burner,
An ash flyer,
A bad screamer,
A mad circular,
A light spinner,
A colour maker,
A slow flyer,
A kid scarer,
A baby crier,
What am I?

(A Catherine wheel)

Harrison Irons (9)
Cliffe Woods Primary School

What Am I? Kennings

A bomb maker
A screaming banshee
A boom maker
An ear piercer
A fire burner
A fizzing ball
A fire filled
A crackling bomber
A sky lighter
A stick launcher
An earth shaker
An eye grabber
A warm feeler
A noise maker
A dog frightener
A pet trembler
A whizzing spinner
A flying shooter
What am I?

(A firework)

Tom Walkinshaw (10)
Cliffe Woods Primary School

What Am I? Kennings

A prey extinguisher
A deer demolisher
A buffalo beater
A desert stalker
A prey pouncer
A monkey muncher
With needle-sharp claws
Skin-tearing teeth
Large, furious, furry
A cunning cat
Soft but masterful
Grey and muscular
Speedy on its pins
A low prowler
A speed breaker.
What am I?

(A lioness)

Lauren Nightingale (10)
Cliffe Woods Primary School

What Am I? Kennings

A good kick-boxer
A fast jumper
A baby carrier
A zoo cager
A veg eater
A big footer
A kiddy scarer
A cage chiller
A hard handler.
What am I?

(A kangaroo)

Joshua Mann (9)
Cliffe Woods Primary School

What Am I?

A bold caller,
A noise shooter,
A grub eater,
A bird dazzler,
An eye catcher,
A jungle diva,
A laughter maker,
A star singer,
A tree pecker,
A wing glider,
A proud beggar,
A smile seeker,
A painful scratcher,
A flow grater,
A star flyer,
A magnificent stroller,
A feather blaster,
A high diver,
A vine grabber.
What am I?
(A parrot)

Sarah Fisher (11)
Cliffe Woods Primary School

The Dover Pincher

There once was a Dover pincher
The pincher's owner was Dover
But when Dover was horrid to the pincher
The pincher pinched him back!

Then once in the old Dover park
The pincher pinched all the bark
He went to a phone, then a no fouling zone
Then was chased by the staff!

James McAllister-Dew (9)
Convent Preparatory School

Oh My!

My mum bought me some glasses
They didn't look nice on me
I sat on these horrid things
Then I had to flee

Then Mum bought me a bow tie
Then trousers length of three quarters
Braces were next
She didn't shop at Bluewaters

Mum had planned more things
According to what I heard
I was upset by my mum
She's turning me into a nerd.

Geevan Binning (10)
Convent Preparatory School

The Mad House

In a mad house, that's where I live
The house is shaped like a sieve
It's awfully damp
It is such a cramp

The pet's a huge chimpanzee
Keeps drinking a cup o' tea
He lives in a hole
Where he met a mole

As for me, I met a bee
Over time it stung me
In fattest cheek

That's the end of me

My dad has a spotted hat
Which makes him look like a cat
Mum is a Bramley
My strange family!

Nicholas Petken (9)
Convent Preparatory School

Desk Wars

A ball of gum and paper
Just flew through the air.
It hit the teacher in the back
And gave her quite a scare.

She turned around quite startled
Her name was Mrs Elly.
She seems to wobble all the time
We call her Mrs Jelly!

She strutted across to my desk.
'Where is Master Bay?'
She couldn't stop this war of grief
It just went on all day!

This seems to happen every year
There's trouble all around.
But when she tells us off like that
We do not make a sound!

We were writing out a poem
About the wooden cane.
I went to get some paper
And did it all again.

So that's how we have desk wars
We argue and argue and fight.
And that is what I dream about
When it strikes midnight.

George Washbourn (10)
Convent Preparatory School

A Limerick For Howard

There once was a boy, name of Howard,
Whose friends wrongly called him a coward,
He liked riding horses,
Who ran round racecourses,
And whose show jumping was really high powered.

Howard Harper (9)
Convent Preparatory School

I Want To Be A Pop Star

I want to be a pop star
And drive a fancy car
With rings on my toes
And a stud in my nose
I know I could go far.

I want to be a pop star
I'd wear expensive clothes
I'd look great
Have loads of mates
And I won't have any woes.

I want to be a pop star
I'd have a fabulous voice
That'd be my choice
I'm cool and I'm tall
Do you think I could be a pop star?

Harsimran Bains (10)
Convent Preparatory School

Battle Of The Kitchen

Apprentices were armed with saucepans
Trudging into battle.
Their opponents used carving knives
(Which set off quite a rattle).

Cooks' assistants destroyed with ladles
Until pushed back by spoon.
Spoonsmen were met without challenge
Until someone threw a prune.

Head chefs wreaked havoc with dishcloths
Breaking enemy rank.
The foe fled back to their kitchen
To be met by a leaky tank.

Ross Homden (9)
Convent Preparatory School

New Girl At School

The sad, miserable girl,
Squashed up near a wall,
Looking blue and mournful.
No one with whom she could play.
I crept up to her, silently.
I approached and sat beside her,
She looked at me and smiled.
I felt she was going to be my friend.

I remembered when I was new,
I didn't even have a friend,
I knew what it felt like,
To be alone.
I wanted to be friends with her,
But I didn't know what to do.
Do you think you can help me?
Please do!

Priya Kumar (10)
Convent Preparatory School

My Poem

My favourite season is summer
I like to go to the park
Play with my friends
Until the day ends
When we pedal off home in the dark

The season I hate is winter
It is all dark and gloom
Through my window I stare
My heart full of care
I don't want to stay in my room.

Yasmine Bance (10)
Convent Preparatory School

Sisters

Waves crash on the sand.
Hand in hand we stroll,
Sisters separated by seas.
Collection of many shells,
Ice creams that we lick and slurp,
Watching the tide slowly ebb.
We don't see each other much
But we still catch up.
She's getting married soon
So then I'll see her again.
But in the meantime
I'm stuck at home
On the other side of the world,
Wishing that we were together!

Amy Jones (10)
Convent Preparatory School

Shyloww And Maddie

I once knew a dog
His name was Shyloww
Who lived in a gynormous mansion
The garden was as big as the night sky
He could play in it all day.

He met a horse called Maddie
They played together all day
When night-time fell
They galloped and pranced
In the long dance all night long.

Chantale Wright (10)
Convent Preparatory School

I Have A Little Sister

I have a little sister
Who wants to be the centre of attention
But all I think she deserves
Is a good long year of detention.

At school she just cries and cries
I don't think she ever stops
So when the cleaner comes at night
She finds she needs a mop!

So when it's finally evening
I go and have a peep
To find that she's not crying
For instead she's fast asleep.

Amrit Khaira (10)
Convent Preparatory School

Holidays

My holiday was boring,
Just like the last!
Why can't we go somewhere 'exciting'
Just like my friends?

I went walking in Wales.
My friend, Shannon, went skiing in Switzerland.
Why can't I go there?
We were going to Mexico
But my dad cancelled.
My friend went to Australia
But my mum said it was *tooooo* far
Just like the last time!
Why can't we go somewhere *'exciting'*?

Katy Nutt (10)
Convent Preparatory School

The Wind Sings

The wind in the trees,
Hummed like the bees.
When the tree sings,
Like a bird's fluttering wings.

I heard wind bellow,
Rustling the meadow.
Grass is whistling,
Like a child whispering.

Nyree MacTavish (10)
Convent Preparatory School

Wintertime

Snowflakes glisten
Falling proud
Gaining speed
Towards the ground.

Icy breezes
Cutting through
Air and fog
To get to you.

Winter sun
Upon your face
Gives no warmth
To this human race.

Children's laughter
Sounding loud
Being playful
All year round.

Wintertime means give a cheer
All year round until it's here
Enjoy it while you can
The winter snow
Until the last moment before it goes!

Kelly Patterson (10)
Elaine Primary School

The Watching Crocodile

The crafty crocodile
Always keeps
One eye open
When the other eye sleeps.

He lies in the river
Pretending to doze
And waits for a fish
To swim past his nose.

Snap! go his jaws
The meal is gone
He smiles and waits
For another one.

Take care little fishes
As you swim by
Remember, remember
The crocodile's eye.

Toni Reynolds (10)
Elaine Primary School

Dolphins

As the dolphin moves to a faraway sea
It is always as playful as it can be
Even still it gets treated badly
It can always swim around lively
They always swim around in one group
Just to be happy and playful
Dolphins are always kind
But people think they are harmful
Just as they are wild
They get a happy life
It is a very helpful animal
It should be treated better.

Alicia Whyte (11)
Elaine Primary School

The 11+

My mouth is dry,
My mind is blank,
My hands are sweaty,
My heart just sank.

I would like a future,
From the exams I take,
I've worked so hard,
Oh, for goodness sake.

I answer the questions,
Slowly, one by one,
Five minutes to go,
Thank goodness, all done.

I sigh with relief,
And walk from the room,
Sure it's all over,
But the results still loom.

I won't look back,
I've done my best,
But I do really hope,
I've passed my test.

Zoe Keating (11)
Elaine Primary School

There's A Boy

There's a boy I like
He's a really cool guy
Whenever I see him
He's always looking fly
The way he gazes into my eyes
I always feel shy
The way he walks
And the way he talks
Make me feel like a million bucks
To go out with a guy so fly.

Ejatu Turay (11)
Elaine Primary School

Roundabout

I was 'ere
And Michael was 'ere
And Gareth snogged Stacie 'ere.
We wrote our names
All around the frames
The swings, the slides, the roundabout.
We used to play
On summer days
Before and after bullying we stayed.
But things have burst
Around with a curse
The swings, the slide, the roundabout.
Now we fart
On the iron bars
Syringes lie on top of cars.
A burnt out see-saw
Lies on the floor
The swings, the slide, the roundabout.
And every day
Is painted gay.
On a dark winter's day
Go scream and swear
Everywhere
The swings, the slide, the roundabout.
Now they play
Our way
Especially that Mary May.
Now we try
To walk by
The swings, the slide, the roundabout.

Stacie Thomas (10)
Elaine Primary School

The Fairy Queen

There is a magical place beyond this world,
Where the fairy queen lives
Where she twirls and whirls.
Where she plays with the kids
And knows all of their names,
Her castle is made out of chocolate fudge,
When people fly by she nudges and shoves,
People say she is the greatest queen of them all,
Only one problem - she is too tall!

Jodie Southgate (10)
Elaine Primary School

Jack Frost

I am what makes your car break down,
And with ice your windows drown,
For I'm mischievous, don't you see?
I am Jack Frost, yes that is me!

I dance across your windowpane,
Do you see that pattern? That symbol's my name
And covering everything in frost is my game.

I am what makes your car break down,
And with ice your windows drown,
For I'm mischievous, don't you see?
I am Jack Frost, yes that is me!

Look very closely, do you see?
That winter wonderland was created by me
And to be King of Winter is my dream.

I am what makes your car break down,
And with ice your windows drown,
For I'm mischievous, don't you see?
I'm Jack Frost, victorious, that's me!

Lizzi Hill (11)
Hilltop Primary School

The A-F Of Bedtime

A is for awake
When you can't get to sleep
So maybe you should go downstairs
But only if you creep

B is for your bed
That lovely thing to sleep in
So grab your teddy and your dog
And anything else you're keeping

C is for the curtains
Remember, shut them tight
For if you look out in the dark
You may get such a fright

D is for the daytime
Which you will wake up to
And if you go to bed right now
The first out could be you

E is for the evening
That's when you go to bed
And you should always go to sleep
Because that's what Mummy said

F is for farewell
Or goodbye you could say
But now it's time to go to sleep
And for me to go away.

Yasmin Brown (10)
Hilltop Primary School

My Sister

She is like a little cloud bursting with joy.
She's like a happy little bunny jumping all around.
She is like a little mouse laughing all the time.
She is like a light bulb switching on and off.

Aimee Newberry (7)
Holy Trinity CE School

What is Heaven?

Is Heaven a place for eternal sleep
Or lifeless souls for him to keep?
    Forever frozen
    Forever dead
Remembering things that they once said
    Forever frozen
    Forever still
Reincarnate at their will
Or is it a place where fire is burning?
Red and evil, the Devil is stirring
Are angels saints with white gowns and wings
Or devils with tails and evil grins?
Is Earth a place of peace and love
Gentle beauty as a graceful dove
Or full of darkness, destruction and gloom?
If we continue this way, we're sure to be doomed.

Toni Ives (11)
Holy Trinity CE School

The Rhythm And The Beat

When the rhythm goes around
The beat comes around
All you need to do is
Stamp your feet and
Jump up and down
Remember just do it in a beat
Turn around and
Clap your hands
Remember do it in a rhythm
When the beat goes around
The rhythm comes around
Feel the beat and feel the rhythm
It's the beat and the rhythm
That gets you off your feet.

Ikra Arshad (10)
Holy Trinity CE School

Snowball Fight

As I look outside
It's snowing
Snowy flakes falling
It's snowing
Everywhere white as a cloud
It's snowing
The golden sun is waking up
It's melting
All the icicles *drip-drop, drip-drop*
It's melting
We go to bed
Is there any magic left?
The next day
It's snowing again
Snowflakes still falling
Come to school on the white blanket
Everyone excited
There's the bell
Snowball fight!

Thomas Uings (10)
Holy Trinity CE School

My Mum

She is a star
A sparkling, beautiful star.
She is like a rainbow in the sky
That flutters through the air.
She's like a polar bear
That cuddles you softly.
She's like a lovely servant
That helps us tidy the house.
She's like a flower
A lovely flower with sun shining on it.

Laura Walton (7)
Holy Trinity CE School

War

People splutter
Children flutter
Women scream
Life's not a dream
Legs moaning
Shelters groaning
Scrabbling, shrieking,
Babbling for their families
Boom, boom, crash.

Smoke flies away
Everyone crying for what happened today
Silence has reigned
The community is spiritually hurt
But peace has arrived
Going to each other
Trying to abide together.

Michael Adeyemo (11)
Holy Trinity CE School

My Mum

She is like a butterfly
Sitting on a leaf.
She is like cotton wool
All soft and fluffy.
She is like a dolly
Lovely and cuddly.
She is like a question mark
That always puzzles me.
She is like my favourite teddy bear
That never forgets me.

Danica Bassoo (8)
Holy Trinity CE School

My Friend

She is like a pony
Running in the clouds.
She is like a pop star
Singing on the stage.
She is like a teacher
Telling us what to do.
She is like the sun in the sky
Shining down on me.
She is like a rainbow
Shimmering in the sky.
She is like a raindrop
Falling to the ground.

Megan Pretious (7)
Holy Trinity CE School

My Friend

She is like a teddy bear
Nice and cuddly.
She is like a princess
Shining in the sky.
She is like a butterfly
Flying around the room.
She is like a bird
Singing in a tree.
She is like a worm
Wriggling underground.
She is like an angel
Floating on a cloud.

Natasha Savage (7)
Holy Trinity CE School

My Friend

She is like a star in the sky
A beautiful star
A gold star
And a shiny star
She is like a happy star
She's like a dancer dancing everywhere.

Ranveer Kaur (8)
Holy Trinity CE School

My Mum

She's like a storm
Roaring at the river.
She is like a swan
Racing through the water.
She's like a happy bunny
Skipping along the path.
She's like a cuddly chair.
She's like a dragon
Getting ready to fire.
She's like a lion
Roaring at a bird.
She's like my sister.

Mohamed Kamara (7)
Holy Trinity CE School

My Teacher

She is like a bird looking for a worm.
She is like a rose losing all her petals.
She is like a dress moving in the wind.
She is like a duck floating in deep blue water.
She is like a polar bear sleeping in the snow.
She is like a roller coaster whizzing round and round.
She is like a blossom falling in the wind.

Amandeep Balrow (8)
Holy Trinity CE School

My Friend Mohit

He is like a cheetah
Looking for his prey.

He is a happy bunny
Jumping up and down.

He is a comfy pillow
In a bed.

He is a golf player
Playing with his stick.

He is a football champion
Running like the wind.

He is a tree
In the wind.

He is a storm
A grumpy lad!

Coyes Nahar (7)
Holy Trinity CE School

My Mum

She is a rose in a tree,
She is in full bloom.
She is like a butterfly,
Zooming through the sky.
She is like a newspaper,
Without new words.
She is like a rose,
Without any thorns.
She is like a pillow,
That I can cradle.
She is like a light bulb,
But not as hot.
She is like a packet of crisps,
But you cannot undo il!

George Pitcher (7)
Holy Trinity CE School

My Mum

She is as warm as wool
Just like the sun.
She is bright
Bright as a rose.
She is anxious
Anxious as a child.
She is a star
Just like silk.
She is huge
Huge as a tree.
She is loud
Loud as a waterfall.
She is pretty
Pretty as a queen.
She is soft
Soft as a river.
She is quiet
Quiet as a mouse.

Christian Fialho (8)
Holy Trinity CE School

My Sister

She is like a fish
Swimming in the water.
She is like a dancer
Dancing all the time.
She is like a cuddly teddy bear
Cuddling everyone.
She is like a cute kitten
Being a princess.
She is a pen
Scribbling everywhere.

Manisha Binning (8)
Holy Trinity CE School

Kidnapping

Peace

Step by step make my way home,
Open the door, my mum's on the phone,
She sends me to the shop to get some bread,
'You'll need a fifty pence,' just like the shop man said,
Strolling through the alley
Back sinking down

Stop!

Hand over my mouth and
I'm trying to breathe,
He's dragging me to the car!
Pounding heart,
Squealing sadly,
Punching, pushing, pulling me badly,
Can't hold much longer!
Dropping to the ground,
It's too late now,
Everything's turning round and round.

Sharanjit Kang (11)
Holy Trinity CE School

My Mum

She is like a star in the sky.
She is like a beautiful diamond up in the tree.
She is like a bee stinging birds.
She is like a teacher in school.
She is like a butterfly in the sky.
She is like a panda jumping with joy.
She is like a rose on the ground.

Shanice Sutherland (7)
Holy Trinity CE School

Nonsense Poem

My numb thumb,
Annoys my mum,
Because it goes big and blue,
Especially when I've got the flu.
My numb thumb,
Annoys my aunt,
Because it makes her seasick,
Especially when I've got the flu.
My numb thumb,
Annoys my dad,
Because it makes him dizzy,
Especially when I've got the flu.
My numb thumb,
Annoys my uncle,
Because he goes *mental*,
Especially when I've got the flu!
                    Achooooo!

Jaye Presland (10)
Holy Trinity CE School

My Teenage Sister

She is like a bunny,
As soft as a bear.
She is like a bird,
Up in the air.
She is like a fire
That keeps me warm.
She is like a tree,
Very tall.
She is my sister,
The best one of all.

Emily Smith (8)
Holy Trinity CE School

The Gale

It had been a silent night
But then suddenly the wind
Awoke,
The gate lay there on
The floor
From the
Thrashing of the wind.
Bin lids had been turned
Everywhere
The slates off the garage had
Flown off
From the thrashing of
The wind
The blare of the
Trees swirling around.
As the wind screeched through its
Branches
The wind sounds like wolves
Howling
As the wind passed
The sun rose and looked
Down.

Jake Bennett (11)
Holy Trinity CE School

My Teacher

She is like a petal falling to the ground.
She is like a feather swimming in the sky.
She is like a panda snuggling down.
She is like a rose drifting in the lake.
She is like a dinosaur roaring for its prey.
She is like a tweety bird singing in the sun.

Prabhdeep Dulay (8)
Holy Trinity CE School

Homelessness

Some people live with family,
Some people are refugees,
Some people live in houses,
Some people live in trees.

I wonder what it feels like,
Some people have had a fight.
Some people argue,
I bet they don't have a light.

Some people stay at home,
Some people run away.
Some people have fun,
Some people come back another day.

Some people sleep on the path,
Some people sleep in a bed.
Some people have dreams,
Some people have things running through their head.

Adam Bassoo (9)
Holy Trinity CE School

My Horrible Friend

She is like a roaring bear
With grizzly hair.

She's a robot
Who's very mean and wicked.

She is like a happy swearing machine,
Swearing every time.

She is like a koala,
Who's eating you.

She is like a lion,
Who hurts my feelings.

Nafeesa Arshad (7)
Holy Trinity CE School

My Brother Of Destruction

My brother is 17 years old,
He does not always do what he is told.
He is a football fan,
He sometimes likes his nan.
From his room loud music you hear,
He must have a blocked ear.
He always calls me up to show me things,
But I wished I had a pair of wings.
He is obsessed with himself,
In the mirror he looks like an elf.
He is big and tall,
He makes me feel small.
He is always in a bad mood,
Sometimes he is rude
And he is always eating too much food.
He's got Craig David's beard
And he really acts weird.
But he is really OK for a brother
And I wouldn't change him for another.

Ajay Singh Bedesha (8)
Holy Trinity CE School

My Aunt

She is beautiful and loving,
Like a rose floating in the air.

She is calm like a river,
Drifting overhead.

She is a diamond of light,
Shimmering in the night.

She is a golden star,
Wandering by.

Rima Khatun (7)
Holy Trinity CE School

King Of The Jungle

He sits among the bushes
Waiting for his prey
The breeze gently pushes
But still he silently lays

He waits for a chance
To quietly prance
Above a bloodthirsty animal
Just like a cannibal

Finally it comes
Its heart beats like a drum
It catches his vicious, hungry eyes
But not one gentle cry

Moving with elegance and grace
It's no longer a race
To be the first to catch a pretty sight
Now in the limelight

Take it in the jaws
Blood dripping more and more
Instantly all gone
Back in the bushes alone.

Lakhmi Halaith (10)
Holy Trinity CE School

My Sister

She is like a bumblebee flying in the sky.
She is like a firecracker exploding in the sky.
She is like a cat standing on the ground.
She is like a monster looking at the sea.
She is like a panda looking in a cave.

Liam Tillman (7)
Holy Trinity CE School

My Mum

She is like a rainbow
Shining in the sky.

She is like a princess of the world
Shimmering in the sunshine.

She is like a rose of light
Shining in the night.

She is like a diamond of sunlight
Shimmering in a rainbow.

She is like a bird
Singing in the tree.

She is a little, happy rabbit
Skipping in a park.

She is like a puppy
Skipping in the park.

Blessings Obideyi (7)
Holy Trinity CE School

My Brothers

They are like a red rose
Dancing in the garden.

They are like a gust of wind
Whistling through the trees.

They are like a fish
Swimming in a pond.

They are like a clown
Juggling in a circus.

They are like a baby bear
Playing in the woods.

Rafet Karabel (70
Holy Trinity CE School

Life

Mum and Dad fighting,
Household problems,
Need to communicate,
      Life.

Children fighting,
Always starting trouble,
Teacher tells off wrong child,
Says he's fair, never is fair,
Dislikes me, I don't care,
Doesn't know my problems,
No one knows my problems,
Don't want to talk,
Don't want to listen,
Don't want to communicate,
      Life.

Go home stressed and confused,
Want to sleep,
No, got work to do,
Time's against me,
Everyone's against me,
Mum, Dad, sisters, brothers, aunts, teacher, children,
      Life.

Farida Tejan (10)
Holy Trinity CE School

My Friend

He is like a tree with no bark,
He is like a drainpipe with no drain.
He's like a door shaking like hair.
He's like a newspaper with no words.
He is a tree with pound note leaves.
He is like a fish swimming with no water.
He is like a nest with no sticks.

Kieran Beveridge (7)
Holy Trinity CE School

Return From The Pub

The driver
Slumps at his wheel in a drunken haze
Through bleary eyes he stares at the road
Only had a couple, he thinks
Can handle my drink.
Painfully shaking his head, he spots a girl
On a bike
She is under the speed limit
He is speeding like a rocket down the road
He cannot brake
He is numb
There is four feet between them
Brain won't respond
She looks into his eyes
Fear, panic, tears
He sees nothing
He hears nothing
Not even two centimetres between them
Crash!
Dead.
But that is only the first.

Jasmin Elliott (10)
Holy Trinity CE School

Mrs Healy

She is a tall giraffe
Eating juicy green leaves.

She is like a cuddly polar bear
All soft and warm.

She is like a beautiful bonfire
Set in a dark sky.

She is like a butterfly
Fluttering in a light blue sky.

Jaskiran Kaur Sodhi (7)
Holy Trinity CE School

A Spelling Lesson

Wanda Witch went wandering,
Within a spooky wood,
She loved to practise spooky spells,
And hated being good.

Wanda turned some bluebells,
Into smelly, slimy goo,
She gave a tree a creepy face,
To scare the likes of *you!*

She crept up on a wizard,
And before he could respond,
Wanda waved her wand
And he fell straight into a pond!

Although it was not very deep,
The wizard soon saw red,
He cast a spell which made his cloak,
Flap right round Wanda's head.

It wrapped around her body
And squeezed her really tight,
'Say sorry,' roared the wizard,
'Or stay like that all night!'

The witch agreed and told him,
'Your magic is so fast,
No more naughty spells from me,
I've really cast my last!'

Pavendeep Kallu (11)
Holy Trinity CE School

Snake

Slithering slowly
Without a sound
Surrounding its scaly self around its supper
Silver scales shine in the sun
Slithering to seek another snack.

Janet Amu (10)
Holy Trinity CE School

My Friend

He is like a cuddly bear.
He is like a soft cushion on the sofa.
He is like a ruby shining in my room.
He is like a rose in the tree.
He is like the wind blowing over my head.
He is like a handsome man standing in my heart.

Chantel Higglesden (7)
Holy Trinity CE School

My Baby Sister

She's like a pretty little baby
Lying in the sun.

She is like a flower
Growing in the park.

She is like a very happy baby with flowers on her dress
And her nose so small.

She is like a bunny
Hopping around.

Noor Chaudhry (8)
Holy Trinity CE School

It's Snowing!

As everybody looks out of the window,
Snow just trickling down.
Everybody running out with their sleighs,
Snow fights in the playground.
The feeling of snow is soft and cuddly,
As the snow touches me, a shiver goes down my spine.

Amandeep Sall (9)
Holy Trinity CE School

The Spirit Of The Sky

With my slender wings I fly above,
With the speed of a jet, the grace of a dove,
My beautiful wings stretch out beside me,
I am so beautiful, no need to hide me,
The clouds as I pass bow down to me,
No humans know what a sight I am to see,
But they still hunt me, capture me and kill me,
Just to use me for their evil deeds.
Their nests, so big and high,
Almost reaching me and the sky,
As I see the mounds of stone I gasp with awe,
But they still bring me and others to war.
I ride through the skies as fast as the night,
I am a spirit, I am a kite.

Kayleigh Brook (10)
Holy Trinity CE School

School

The bell is ringing
For school to begin.
The doors have just opened
The children rush in.
Knocking over teachers
Hurting little kids,
Rushing to and fro
Flicking pen lids.

The bell is ringing
For children to go.
Peace through the school.
The children all rush
Out of the doors,
Out of the gates
Looking for the place
Where their parents wait.

Nardeep Manu (11)
Holy Trinity CE School

Molly And Meg

Molly and Meg went to the zoo
And this is what they saw
Two monkeys running all over the place
And a clumsy kangaroo.

Molly and Meg went to the zoo
And this is what they saw
Two tigers chasing a manic man
And a kangaroo shouting *boo!*

Molly and Meg went to the zoo
And this is what they saw
Two enormous elephants blowing their horns
And dolphins going *moo!*

Molly and Meg went to the zoo
And this is what they saw
A hissing snake, which loved to bake
And detectives not having a clue

Molly and Meg went to the zoo
And this is what they saw
This terrible place, which they thought was an ace
And ran out with a zoom.

Elizabeth Olaniyan (11)
Holy Trinity CE School

Cats And Dogs

C urtains are used as ladders,
A nd sofas are used as scratch mats,
T ogether cats use these well,
S ometimes cats use these too much.

D ogs can be rough,
O ther dogs can be nice,
G rowling all day long,
S currying for food.

Nicolle Marshall (10)
Holy Trinity CE School

Tigers

Tigers have stripes,
Orange and black.
They live in jungles
And creep up to their prey.
They teach each other how to fight,
They never lose but always win.
They scare nearly everything,
Everything, including me.

Anna Rolfe (9)
Holy Trinity CE School

What I Like The Most

What I like the most
Is to lick the strawberry sauce off my ice cream
It is to drink from a fresh stream

What I like the most
Is to swim in the sea
It is to go down a ride and say, *'whoopee!'*

What I like the most
Is to see all of the sights
It is to look at the Christmas lights

But what I like the most is just to be me!

Chianne Bal (10)
Holy Trinity CE School

Bomb!

People running
People screaming
Children crying
Children screaming
The world is not safe anymore
So what shall we do?

Samia Chaudhry (10)
Holy Trinity CE School

Colin The Cat's Everyday Life

Colin gets up, eats breakfast,
Sleeps.
Wakes up, eats lunch, chases a mouse,
Sleeps.
Goes into the garden, makes himself comfy,
Sleeps.
Gets his tail trodden on, eats tea,
Sleeps.
Goes for a walk, goes back to bed,
Sleeps.
What a lazy cat Colin is!
Night-time comes, terrorist cat,
Sprays on prize plants,
Scratches up fences,
Screams all night long,
Early morning, goes back to bed,
Sleeps.

Eleanor Webb (10)
Holy Trinity CE School

Books

Books,
Words,
Pages,
Sentences,
Paragraphs,
All these things in books.

Full stops,
Commas,
Apostrophes,
Question marks,
Exclamation marks,
Speech marks,
Punctuation in those books,
Wow, all these things in books.

Joseph Lima (9)
Holy Trinity CE School

Ghost!

Ghost is coming, he is coming in the door,
He is wrecking the house,
He is slowly passing your cat,
He is going up the stairs into your bedroom.
There is a *boom!* as you locked your door,
You hooked your bungee rope on the window,
You hope you will be safe,
You climb down the window,
You're safe in the garden,
Ghost is there following you,
Ghost has finally given up chasing you.

Freya Penfold (9)
Holy Trinity CE School

The Ghost That Lived At The Post

Once upon a time there lived a ghost
Who had to live at the post
He and his family were incredibly shocked
So they sent him to be docked.
They sent him to Dover Castle
All wrapped in a brown parcel!
Then came back
And ran to Iraq

He joined the army
But in the sun
He went quite barmy
He ranted and raved
Attention he craved!
They put him on the stage
He became the rage
The most famous ghost in the Milky Way!

He had a concert in May
And then moved away
And was never heard of again.

Jamie Watson (11)
Kings Farm Primary School

The Stupid Ghost

T heodopolous was a stupid ghost
H e had no brain, he liked to boast
E very day he would shout and scream

' S pecially when he had a dream
T hat evening he went to the park
U ntil he got scared of the dark
P eople thought he was just stupid and sad
I nstead he was just a little bit mad
D opley was his friend, and used to make him happy

G eorge was a grumpy ghost who wore a big fat nappy
H allowe'en was a favourite time for him
O ver the hill lived a cool ghost who had a dog
S napping, barking, horrible thing
T ook it for walks on a piece of string.

Giuseppe Trimarco (11)
Kings Farm Primary School

The Ghost Who Choked On His Toast

There once was a ghost
Who choked on his toast
He was so angry
And really hungry
Because he couldn't scare
Because he was bare.
He broke a chair
Because he had no hair.
It was bright.
He had a fright.
He was white
Because his pants were tight.
He had a bit at night.
That poor old ghost who choked on his toast.

Luke Todd (11)
Kings Farm Primary School

The Fat Ghost Called Lee

There was a fat ghost called Lee,
Who found a magic key.
It led to a mountain,
Which had a dazzling fountain.
He bumped into a tree,
Because he couldn't see!

He fell down a drain,
But wasn't in pain!
He was going insane,
Because of food - glorious food!

He popped up again, this time in a pie,
He tried to eat as much as he could.
But would it go in?
No - it usually would!
But not this time.
You can still hear him whine!
You will till the end of time.
That skinny ghost called Lee.

Michael McGrath (10)
Kings Farm Primary School

The Funny Ghost

F red the ghost lived in a house
U nder the stairs with a mouse
N o one can see him during the day
N ight is his favourite time to play
Y ou have got to believe to see him.

He's got a friend called Jim
They had a party on a boat
Over the top of a goat
Silly old Fred
Told Jim to go to bed
Silly old Fred wet the bed.

Natasha Newstead & Kirsty Morris (11)
Kings Farm Primary School

Love Never Dies

Love is like candles in the wind
It starts like a weak flicker and gets stronger.
It may be blown out
Unless someone relights it.

True love never dies
It leaves its mark in your heart
It warms you like a candle.

True love never dies
You may be young,
Love leaves its mark.

I shall never forget
My loved ones
Neither shall you.

The memory of love is like stars,
Comes out at night,
And lives in your dreams
You may not see them but they are always there.

Megan Osbourne (9)
Kings Farm Primary School

Fireworks

F ireworks are all different colours
I n the dark night sky
R ed, blue, purple and orange are my best
E very rocket shooting up high
W hirling fireworks going round and round up
    to the midnight sky
O n the burning bonfire
R ests Guy Fawkes
K eeping the flames red-hot
S o when the fireworks are over everyone goes home.

Kirsty Addison (9)
Kings Farm Primary School

Spooky Yard At Midnight . . .

S pooky noises in the graveyard
P eople dead walk around
O ff they set to the places
O nce where they lived
K nocking on doors
Y ear after year.

Y ikes! After they died they all
A wakened and went out to
R uin the places where they
D ied of all different things.

A t midnight whey they were alone they sing softly
T hen the dead sing aloud.

M urder, murder, murder!
I n the night!
D ead down, dead now!
N o one can help us!
I, we have no life!
G od help us, bring us back!
H elp us!
T he dead cry.

Jodie Hamilton (10)
Kings Farm Primary School

It's Raining Cats And Dogs

One wet day in the forest,
It was raining cats and dogs
And when they landed on the ground
They jumped over the logs
The cats and dogs race each other,
To and fro through the trees
Through the flowers
Being chased by the bees.

Amber Boyle (10)
Kings Farm Primary School

Friends

Friends are there
Through thick and thin,
Friends are there
To help you win,
Friends are there,
By your side,
Friends are there
To share your pride.

Corrigan Hicks (10)
Kings Farm Primary School

The Car

The bright blue Rover
Sits in the dazzling sun
In a street in Dover
It likes to go for a nice long run
Past the bright fields of clover
    Having great fun!

Charlie Pankhurst, Mathew Arney & Michael Newstead (9)
Kings Farm Primary School

Aliens

A liens live in outer space
L anding on the moon
I ntelligence far beyond the human brain
E verywhere they go they scare people away
N otorious for being shocking
S ailing the solar system in their ships.

McKayla Cullen (9)
Kings Farm Primary School

Kings Farm Colts

K ings Farm are better than Spartens
I n the cup we beat them 12-0
N ext match we thrashed them 36-1
G ame was in the night
S tormy night the match was played.

F ootball fans fought
A nd cheered for Farm
R acing up and down the pitch
M y mum celebrated for me for playing so well.

C an we win it? Yes we can!
O ur team celebrated for winning the cup
L oads of us got cups given out
T hen all of us went home
S o we went home and had a bath.

Craig White (9)
Kings Farm Primary School

My Rollerblades

I love these things, they're bright and colourful,
They come in different shades,
I can do all kinds of tricks on them,
I call these things my rollerblades.

I go up different sized ramps,
With my helmet on
Performing 50-50 rails
And I never go wrong.
Welcome to the world of rollerblading,
I enjoy my hobby because it's fun
Racing people down the hill
I mostly do it in the sun.

George Parker (10)
Kings Farm Primary School

Family And Friends

I've got a friend called Lisa she is very nice
Me and Lisa eat curry and rice
She comes to knock for me every day before school
She is very cool!
My family like her very much
She tries to stay in touch
Lisa eats pizza and so do I
We can touch the sky
Lisa is eight and I'm coming up nine
We both like shopping all the time
My family are loud they make me very proud
Lisa's family are quiet, we always get in a fight
My family are always awake they are skinny like a rake
Lisa's family are fat and they've got a staff
Me and Lisa are the best of friends.

Which now brings me to my poem's end.

Amy McGrath (9)
Kings Farm Primary School

Motorbikes

Out at the fort, Jack and Jack
Ride their KX80's
Wearing their helmets, boots and gloves
Not forgetting their body armour.

Over the jumps, flying high
Using powerbands and gears.
Mud flying everywhere.
While they are performing doughnuts.

Racing other bikes round a circuit.
The air filled with loud screaming noises.
The smell of petrol lingering there
It's Sunday morning yet again.

Jack O'Brien & Jack Parker (10)
Kings Farm Primary School

Silly Ghost

Here comes the ghost
With lots of toast
So let's make the most
Before night falls.
Hurrying for his favourite meal
Now he's ready to haunt you too.
So hurry now he's going insane
So here I am being a pain.

Amanda Williams (10)
Kings Farm Primary School

Spring

In spring baby lambs are born
There are lots of new flowers
When the lambs wake they yawn
And sometimes are wet by showers.

They cut crops near the rocks
To feed the sheep all year
Every night he shuts the locks
To keep them safe and near.

Maria Watkins (9)
Kings Farm Primary School

The Snake Man

The snake man comes out for a feast
And the roar in the night
Gives the child a fright.
Splattering guts around the room
Everywhere gloom and doom
As the sun comes up the snake man is gone
And all you hear is his faint
Hiss.

Danny Caller (10)
Kings Farm Primary School

Spooky Lady

Down on the motorway at ten past two
Came a pretty lady, eye's bright blue.

Singing a lullaby into the air
Transforming a crowd for her to scare.

The lady flutters to the front of the crowd
Mumbling to herself then singing aloud.

The crowd turns round and follows the song
Down to the beach with the horrible mong.

The lady sweeps the people into the sea
Laughter fills the air as the lady laughs with glee.

Then she says the words that no one hears
Walks into the fog and disappears.

Kirsty Rea (10)
Kings Farm Primary School

Fireworks

Fireworks go high
Into the cold sky
Don't get hurt
There's lots of dirt
Wrap up warm
Hope there's not a storm
Whizzing, screaming, sparkling, shooting and banging
A guy on the bonfire - hanging
Rocket, Roman candles, Catherine wheels and sparklers
That make all different colours
Making shapes wearing gloves
The moon is shining up above.

Jessica Whyman (10)
Kings Farm Primary School

Pandora's Box

There was a girl called Pandora,
She opened a big chest;
The evil in the chest saw her,
The chest was evil's nest.

Disease, cruelty, pain and old age
Pandora trapped little hope;
To hope the chest a cage
The large world could not cope.

She felt so guilty for the world,
She had started to cry;
She sat down on a mat and curled,
So sad she had to lie.

Pandora heard a tiny voice,
The voice she heard was scant;
To let hope free was not a choice
Small hope looked like ant.

Naomi Holmes (9)
Kings Farm Primary School

A Ghost

A fallen shadow on the stairs
Of something that isn't there
A chill, a mist, a haze,
A flash of light
And in amazement
I realise a shape of a man
From years gone by
Soon it's gone
The past was here
But *not* for long.

Jemma Frodsham (10)
Kings Farm Primary School

Creepy Ghost

C reepy ghost running around
R oaring, jumping, a creepy sound
E veryone around horrified and scared
E veryone around terrified and glared
P eople killing people dying
Y ou won't hurt me because you're crying

G hosts can't hurt us, you might think
H ow they nick your blood to drink
O n your own in the night
S keletons and ghosts, give you a big fright
T errifying, horrifiying, nasty noise let's rip up
                    Your bodies boys!

Steven Coleman (10)
Kings Farm Primary School

Alone In The Dark

Alone in the dark
I heard my dog bark
I looked up from my bed
And something was dead.

I stepped on the floor
It opened, its jaw
I ran to the door
And fell to the floor.

I screamed for my dad
Then thought I was mad
I thought it was not there
When I woke up, it was time for the fair.

Jessica Nunnery (10)
Kings Farm Primary School

The Fox And The Crane

A sneaky little fox he was,
And there was a big crane;
Fox invited the crane to tea,
His house was up the lane.

The fox said to the crane, 'Come round,'
The crane said, 'That is fine,'
He saw his house like a hound,
Crane pressed the doorbell chime.

The crane could not get any food,
The fox was laughing like mad;
But the crane was not nasty or rude,
But the crane was very sad.

The crane invited fox to tea,
Fox pointed with his thumb;
The fox said, 'What do you mean me?'
'Yes, would you like to come?'

The fox went to crane for tea,
Crane played a little trick;
The fox could not reach any tea,
Fox was angry and sick.

And the fox went home very mad,
And the crane was laughing;
Don't like it! Don't make others sad,
Then you will be laughing.

Joe Loft (9)
Kings Farm Primary School

Peace

Peace is blue and is the colour of water
It smells like beautiful flowers
It tastes like a hot pizza
It feels like love and joy
It lives in our hearts.

Joseph Holderness (10)
Kings Farm Primary School

Nasty Things

It is a nasty orangey colour
It smells like a volcano burning up
It tastes like rotten tomatoes
It sounds like thunder
It feels like gunge
It lives everywhere.

Jemma Evans (10)
Kings Farm Primary School

Horror Train

G hosts are coming
H orror train
O n the horror track
S it down now
T he train is roaring, it's so horrified

T error ghost
R unning around
A head is coming now
I t's in your bag
N ot at all.

       Don't believe me you silly fool.

Natasha Sutton (10)
Kings Farm Primary School

Hallowe'en Night

One Hallowe'en night there was a howling wind
Bats were hanging in their gloomy caves
Witches, cauldrons, bubbling potions
Werewolves hunting for their prey
So beware take good care
Vampires waking to suck people's blood.

Emma-Louise Coomber (9)
Kings Farm Primary School

Beauty And The Beast

There was a young girl called Beauty,
Her lucky number nine,
She was such a lovely cutie
She was so very fine.

She liked drinking very good wine,
She lived in a castle,
She had very high walls to climb,
She liked having parcels.

One day she went to the forest,
She rode such a nice horse,
Met a boy called Morris,
He showed her a horse course.

The next day the boy Morris died,
Beauty was very sad,
Beauty started to hide and cry,
She said a sad goodbye.

Beauty rode her horse to a house,
She saw an ugly beast,
She saw a very tiny mouse,
Mouse cooked her a nice feast.

The beast took her to his castle,
She fell in love with him,
They had kids and they were rascals,
Chucked nappies in the bin.

Beauty and the beast got married,
Another child they had,
Beauty loved carrying the boy,
Their life was very good.

Henry Eastwood (10)
Kings Farm Primary School

Witch's Recipe

Boiling pot
Slimy frogs
Owl's head chopped off
Bloody fingers in the pot
Vampire teeth in the pot
Snake's tongue in the pot
Slimy eyes
Heart cut in half
Bats flying around the pot
Ghost flying round and round
The witch is coming argh!
What a horrible recipe.

Emmanuella Torto-Doku (9)
Kings Farm Primary School

A Witch's Recipe

A cauldron of cats' claws
Dog's hair
Tabby cat's fur coat
Toad's feet
Dog's tail
Cat's hair
Goldfish
Man-eating shark
Man-eating fish
Wizard's cloak
Bag of flower
A bag of paper
A bag of plastic
What an evil recipe.

Amy Evans (10)
Kings Farm Primary School

Vampire

V isiting witches in the sky
A ll dark, scary night
M ansion's door creaking
P eople screaming
I nvisible noises all around
R ed dragon breathing fire
E veryone scared.

Alan Josh (9)
Kings Farm Primary School

Snot Head Monster

He has a big spike and is two feet tall,
He has big fangs, watch him creeping up the wall.
With his curdling and hairy face
He is sure to scare you all.

He pulls out the brains through the nose,
Its loud howling noise makes the body cut in half,
And the heart jumps out for him to devour.

So I would stay away from the monster if I was you,
        Snot Head.

Andrew Perry (8)
Kings Farm Primary School

Spooky Jade

Beware of Spooky Jade
She will pull your brain out of your nose
And suck the blood from your toes
I will tell you to go away
It's safer near me during the day
I will strike you with my lasers blue
Then have a good chew.

Jade Gibbons (8)
Kings Farm Primary School

Hallowe'en

H allowe'en is scary
A ghost is on its way
L ittle devils are scary
L ittle pumpkins are smelly
O h no, here comes a vampire
W aiting at the door and creaking floor
E asy wolves and dwarves
E very night they come and breathe
N ights are scary.

Keelley Caller (9)
Kings Farm Primary School

The Hairy Beast

Beware of the hairy beast,
He will cook you for his big feast.
Watch out he will be coming for you.
He's going to have a big chew.
The beast will look you in the eye.
Watch out for him in the big blue sky.

Carly Addison (8)
Kings Farm Primary School

The Demon Vampire

Stay away from the demon vampire,
He searches for victims from the church spire.

He will use a hook to pull out your brain, and
Suck blood from your body, in the pounding rain.

He'll grind you to a pulp and swallow you like spaghetti hoops.
Gobble, gobble, gulp for the next course - eyeball soup.
Gobble, gobble, gulp.

For his pudding he scoffs intestines and blood,
Then cleans his teeth in boggy mud.

Kieran Harvey (8)
Kings Farm Primary School

The Troll

The troll is as gooey as snot,
he'll spike you and chuck you in his pot.

So watch out for the old gooey troll
who lives in the dark damp hole.

He'll crunch on your bones and suck your blood,
and wash it all down with some mud.

Gianluca Trimarco (8)
Kings Farm Primary School

Cross Bone Jack

Beware of the crazy cross bone,
Whose real name is Jack Sparrow,
For being a terrible pirate he is known
He is very shallow.

On his cheek he has a scar,
On his ship he travels far.
Stealing goods and fighting with swords
While looking for gold and silver in hoards.

Reece Whyman (9)
Kings Farm Primary School

Mike

Mike the monster looks really slimy
His head is big and round.

Spikes come out of his fingers
Beware in case he touches you.

He will pull your eyeballs out
And boil you up like soup.

Marc Hoad (8)
Kings Farm Primary School

Kings Farm Colts

K ings Farm are better than Spartons.
I n the cup we beat them 12-0.
N ext match we thrashed them 36-1.
G ame was played in stormy night.
S coreboards hidden from sight.

F ootball fans were fighting
A nd cheering for the Farm.
R acing to get the ball
M y mum gave me money for playing well.

C an we win the cup? Yes we can.
O ur team got trophies
L oads of us big trophies
T hey all went home
S o I got up in the morning and had a bath.

Kenny Watkins (10)
Kings Farm Primary School

Alien

Beware of the alien with blood
running down his face.

He is so evil, he's been banned
from space.

He has sharp teeth which can cut
through any meat.

He is filled with squirty water which
is always leaking through his feet.

Although he is evil he always tries to
keep neat.

Jack Andrew (8)
Kings Farm Primary School

Neil The Monster

He is scary and spooky
Sometimes vicious.

With eyes which are frightening
And a heart of wood.

Nails made of spikes
Hair made of nails.

Shelby Clare (8)
Kings Farm Primary School

The Boxing Beast

The boxing beast, he will jump to the moon
and come back down wearing a nightgown.
He sleeps upside down on his bed
resting on his big head.
He looks like a pile of hair
and he swears
has horns and corns
he will come to you at dawn
so stay inside away from his lawn.

Alexander Williams (9)
Kings Farm Primary School

Spiky The Monster

His head is square with an Afro,
He has three red and blue legs with spiky toenails,
And at the end of each leg and arm there are five scary nails.
He has ears the size of an elephant's ears,
He has fangs like a vampire,
And three red eyes and a square body with four arms coming out of it.

Jack Howard (8)
Kings Farm Primary School

The Evil Karate Girl

Beware of the evil karate girl.
She will knock you out with a kick and a swirl.
She will suck anybody's blood
And will smack you with a *bam bam boom.*
In one hit you will be on the floor knocked out
Spikes coming out of her head, legs and arms.
If you see this vicious girl, you have been warned
To stay clear.

William Johnson-Cole (8)
Kings Farm Primary School

Wind

Wind oh beautiful wind
How do you fly so high?
A gentle breeze above the trees
The trees sway in the wind.

Taylor Nightingale (8)
Kings Farm Primary School

Ten Animals

One octopus ordering owls.
Two tyrannosaurus rex thumping.
Three turtles travelling to the tree.
Four fishes frolicking friendly.
Five frogs finding fish.
Six snakes slivering slowly.
Seven swans swimming serenely.
Eight elephants eating eggs.
Nine newts napping.
Ten tigers terrifying toucans.

Emily Davis (8)
Kings Farm Primary School

Pirates Of The Caribbean

Jack Sparrow, a pirate of the Caribbean,
and a lover of rum.
Jack is rather dumb.
He used to be the captain of the Black Pearl.
In the moonlight the crew are cursed.
Clearly from Hell, they make toenails curl.
When it's time to fight, out of the sea they burst.

Jack Sparrow wastes his shot,
but with the help of William Turner,
they defeat the crew from Hell,
and Jack gets back the Pearl.

Charlotte-Marie Garland (9)
Kings Farm Primary School

The Karate Beast

He looks like a beast
He has sharp horns and teeth
When he goes to a party he needs a leash
He eats men and a lot of breath.

He jumps up to the sky
He has a friend called Barty
He comes back down with a shepherd's pie
He got another friend called Marty.

He creeps through thick woods
He has a lot of goods
He's very angry so he eats a boy
And then he plays with the boy's toys.

Ricky Gardner (9)
Kings Farm Primary School

Tales Of The Dead

The water whispered as they passed,
A crescent moon hung in the dark.
While somewhere in the blackened night,
The secret was broken, though all lips stayed shut tight.

And by the signs which were given to him,
He galloped down to the barred up inn.
And stepping through the squelchy mud,
He found her drenched in her own red blood.

And in the tears that he wept and cried,
He rode back grim, with the one who died.

He proclaimed to the public,
That the rumours had been true.
And with that person locked and barred,
He found the only thing to do.

That night he killed him,
Although he denied it,
The only soul who committed the crime -
And with that they left it there,
And the body they buried with care.

Annamarie Tarr (10)
Meopham CP School

Goose On The Loose

A goose called Bruce,
Escaped on the loose,
And went missing for days on end,
Then he bumped into his friend
And said, 'What are you doing here?
I thought you got shot.'
So his friend said, 'Of course not,
I got locked in a barn,
Away from harm,
So go now and I hope we meet again.'
This all sounded insane
He bought some wine,
He began to dine,
He ordered some fish,
It came on a large dish.
He ate some bonbons with it,
He got so drunk he fell down a pit,
So that was the end of the goose
Called Bruce that escaped on the loose!
So if you see him give me a *shout!*

Charlotte Clayton (10)
Meopham CP School

Tiger Tiger

Tiger, tiger proud and right
Tiger, tiger hunting at night
Tiger, tiger took a flight
Tiger, tiger turning white
Tiger, tiger fly a kite
Tiger, tiger leaping right
In the middle of the night.

Lewis Atkinson (9)
Raynehurst Junior School

All About Me

I am a young girl aged only ten
And here my poem will begin
I have a brother who is a pain
And tomorrow he will annoy me again.

My mum says that we are nearly the same
My dad says we can be a pain
I am very strong willed and I will do well in school
And the job I get will be very cool.

My friends are very important to me
And when we play I feel so free
We also share our pain and woe
Then looking forward to tomorrow, off we go.

My mum likes to go out and Dad likes to stay in
We are one great happy family with lots of love within
Here my poem comes to an end
As I said I'm a girl of ten.

Paige Martin (10)
Raynehurst Junior School

My Feathery Friend

My bird is flying up to the tree
Landing on the treetop green
Pulling on the leaves so juicy
Where is she now? Nowhere to be seen.

Found her! Now where's she going?
Spreading her gorgeous wings for winter
Pure white feathers evenly flowing
I wish she wasn't a migrater.

Elizabeth McDonnell (11)
Raynehurst Junior School

Home

Home, home sweet home
Sitting in the pool
Running through the hall
All nice and cool.
Chilling in the mall
Waiting for a call,
Mansion so tall,
I love my home sweet home.

Jade Simpson (9)
Raynehurst Junior School

Trees

Is it a tree I think I can see?
It is so much bigger than me.
Is it a branch there over my head?
Will it die like my mum said?
Is it a leaf falling down?
It's red, it's green, it's kind of brown.
Is it a squirrel and a bird?
A small bat came in third.
Do the trees fall down and die,
Or do they grow back twice as high?

Robert Bussey (11)
Raynehurst Junior School

Haiku

The dog was lying
He said he was sick, he lied
His mother found out.

Alex Wake (8)
Raynehurst Junior School

Valentine's Day

For everyone around you,
For everyone you see,
There's love between us two
I said it's you and me,
Send a card,
I'll love you lots,
It must be hard
But send a box of chocs.

Shannon Presland (8)
Raynehurst Junior School

Our School

O ut to play we go
U nder the friendship tree we chat
R ather exciting, loads to do

S chool is fantastic
C lubs galore
H ope we don't get homework
O h no another test
O utside we do PE
L ater, I'll see you tomorrow.

Gemma Holdoway (11)
Raynehurst Junior School

Market Dog

There was a dog,
eating a chocolate log,
on the way to market,
he found a red basket,
it had a nice big bone in it,
he took it home,
to turn it into a doggy comb.

Daniel Jackson (9)
Raynehurst Junior School

Parrot

I have a parrot who's cheeky
He likes a hug
He likes a cherry
He sleeps in a mug.

He has a little mate (boy)
They squabble
He likes to paint
But when his knees begin to wobble
He goes to a corner
To rest his sleepy head
He's a snorer
When it's time for bed.

James Thomas (9)
Raynehurst Junior School

The Little Bee

There was a little bee
Who lived at the top of a tree
He rested on a branch
Where he could see all the plants.
The flowers smelt very nice
So he went down for pollen twice.
When his tummy was full
He started to drool.
He felt weepy
Because he was sleepy.
This little bee was called Pee-Wee
He was the bee who lived in the tree.

Jessica Bard (11)
Raynehurst Junior School

Friends Haikus

Friends are wonderful
They will never let you down
They will be helpful.

A friend is special,
They are always there for you,
It's good to make friends.

They make you smile wide
They will never be nasty,
They won't make you cry.

They will always care,
A friend can give you a hug,
So make a friend now.

Amy Spillett (9)
Raynehurst Junior School

The Birds

A snow-white dove
That flies high above
With a flick of a wing
And the eye of a dove
To show us all peace
And to show us all love.

A sparrow sits in my garden
Just eating worms all day
That poor little sparrow
Meets the cat, then gets chased away.

Samuel Davis-Dalton (9)
Raynehurst Junior School

The Tale Of The Mysterious Cat!

I sit and stare
At the cat beside me,
With a luminous glare,
And I smile straight at thee.

I sit and try,
To work out what
It's thinking
But all I can see
Are its eyes blinking.

A playful creature
This wonderful thing
As I roll its ball
On a piece of string.

I give it its food
And lay down its bed
It goes out the back,
After it is fed.

I wonder what
Sort of mischief it brings,
While in the back garden,
I pick up its things.

What a wonderful
Marvellous, mischievous cat,
Who follows me to bed,
And dreams happily of rats.

I leave you with this message
To all human beings,
That cats should not be mistreated,
For doing wrong things!

Shanice Faber (10)
Raynehurst Junior School

If You Hide

In the field . . .
Where we play
If you hide . . .
I'll seek you
If you run . . .
I'll catch you
If you get hurt
I'll heal you
When the sun sets . . .
We'll watch it together
And together we'll go home and never
Leave each other's side.

Kayleigh Tyler (11)
Raynehurst Junior School

Snowman Is Frosty

Snowman is frosty,
Snowman is cold,
Snowman has a big orange nose.

I can put a hat on him,
I can put a scarf
I can put some buttons on him
I think he's rather smart.

When the sun comes up
He won't be here to stay
So snowman please come back
Another day.

Jodie Dixon (10)
Raynehurst Junior School

The Three Little Pigs

The three little pigs
Went to the town,
Jumping and dancing all around.
Along comes a fox,
Who jumped on a box,
To scare the pigs away.
The three little pigs
Went to the woods,
Clutching sticks to make a mix,
Along comes a fox to scare them away.

Kayleigh Hilbert (9)
Raynehurst Junior School

Bob The Dog

Bob the dog
Found a frog
Sitting by the pool
But he couldn't stay and play,
He had to go to school.

Bobby Akers (9)
Raynehurst Junior School

Home Sweet Home

Home, home,
My sweet home.
My sweet home is very, very neat.
My sweet home
Home has got a beat
Dancing feet it's very neat.
My home is called Gnome
I love my spinning home
I lost my beat using my feet.

Jade South (9)
Raynehurst Junior School

The Bionic Boy

It really fills me full of joy to be the first bionic boy.
I know that I have got the power to run at sixty miles an hour.
Rope a steer or buffalo or tie a steel rod in a bow.
Stop traffic in a stand by waving my bionic hand.
Knock down trees and break out of jail and fight successfully
with a whale.

But there's just one thing I can't explain
I have not got a bionic brain
and here's something I can't keep to myself
I have no A Levels yet.

Lee Johnson (10)
Raynehurst Junior School

The Griffin

Down came the fastest flyer
Out of his mouth came the brightest fire.
He had very sharp claws, then he opened his jaws
He had a belly that wobbled like jelly.

Joshua Armitage (7)
Raynehurst Junior School

You

Did you know that God above
Created you for me to love
He brought you down from all the rest
Because he knew I'd love you the best.
I had a heart and it was true,
But now it's gone from me to you.
Look after it as I have done
For you have two and I have none.

Chelsea Swain (7)
Raynehurst Junior School

I Can See . . .

Angels sleep
While people peep
Volcanoes start
It looks like art
It is war
Down falls the door
The clouds are black
I see a rat
There is a light
The horse will bite
Boy in blue
What should we do
The horse is running
Isn't he cunning?
Old lady walks
She looks like a stalk
Babies creep
They look like sheep
The ground is rough
It looks like stuff.

Maria McCann (9)
Riverview Junior School

I Can See . . .

The clouds are dark and deep,
While up in Heaven the angels peep
Glowing, shiny, milky stars
Stars like glowing Mars
Flowers growing proper mad
The horse is glowing sad.

Emma Bailey (9)
Riverview Junior School

I Can See . . .

The clouds are dark for all is night
The children get the biggest fright

The night is dark for some to see
But if you do you need a wee

The grow and grow and grow of anger
Keeps the sadness to always linger

The people say I'll get a night
but in the end they get a fright

I think I'm a sieve
But that man will live

The monkey is chunky
And a person is funky.

Conor Lawlor (8)
Riverview Junior School

I Can See . . .

The sky is very misty bright
It's waiting to catch the light.

I'm on a bright, gleaming horse
We're waiting to win a course.

The volcano is erupting red
While me and monkey are eating bread.

I see a horse that leaps up high
And tries to touch the light blue sky.

Jemima Smith (8)
Riverview Junior School

I Can See . . .

The horse is still awake dancing and leaping
And everyone's all tucked in dreaming and sleeping.

The grandma with her child are blowing away
And the sky is going mighty grey.

The children are shouting, 'Hooray, hooray.'
For they like it when the sky is grey.

The sky is oozing out on full power
And growing in size by the hour.

The lava is going away, hooray!
I think it's going to carry on every day.

The smoke is pink
And it looks like coloured ink.

Olivia Lawson (8)
Riverview Junior School

I Can See . . .

On he goes on the bumpy ground
Skeletons pass all around.
Ghosts fly by, witches too
Children will not get home until half-past two
The cats and dogs are running away
The ghosts and ghouls are chasing each day
The horse is running up the hill
The children start to feel a bit ill
As the sky is eroding
The volcano is exploding
The sky is thundering
And the people are wondering.

Sara Port (9)
Riverview Junior School

I Can See . . .

The cloud on Earth in a deep sleep
While the angels are having a wonderful peep.

I said to myself, 'I might have a night'
But instead had an awful fright.

The horse is asleep
The man is a creep.

I thought I was a king
But that was the thing.

The puppy had a bone
But the dog would just groan.

The monkey is chunky
The person is funky.

Kevin Richardson (9)
Riverview Junior School

I Can See . . .

The clouds are gathered, dark and deep
While up in Heaven the angels creep.
The horse is leaping in the air
While a lady just stands there.
The volcano is erupting, everyone is scared
With smoke gathering up in the air
The cottage has lots of light
And the horse is very bright
The grass is very deep
While insects are fast asleep
The volcano is full of lava
It is such a palaver.

Kayleigh Harwood (8)
Riverview Junior School

I Can See . . .

The horse is galloping up the hill
While cats and dogs are chasing their meal.

Boys and girls are playing in the fields
While mums and dads are paying bills.

Hungry children are making their fill
Babies and children going to kneel.

Robbers and thieves are going to steal
And mums and dads are making deals.

Jed Gamman (8)
Riverview Junior School

I Can See . . .

I can see a horse that leaps up high
It leaps so high it touches the sky

The clouds are red like a rose's petal
As they go over the hills and start to settle.

Hazel Williams (8)
Riverview Junior School

I Can See . . .

The horse is going really mad
I think this hour is badly bad

The clouds are coming by and near
Grandma is coming to have a peer

The ground is coming very rusty
It might be very dusty

The horse is going clippety-clop
The boy had a look at the clock

The horse will not settle down
The monkey runs around and around.

Holly Richardson (8)
Riverview Junior School

I Can See . . .

The horse is spotty
And the children go potty
I saw a man
Who looked like your gran.

I saw a house
Which looked like a mouse
I saw a road
Which looked like a load
The clouds are gathered dark and deep
While cats and dogs go to sleep
Babies creep
While we eat
Volcanoes erupt
For a piece of art
A bat
Is fat
The wings
Are things.

Holly Windsor (9)
Riverview Junior School

I Can See . . .

The horse has got dark grey spots
They look like splattered dots.

The clouds are dark and very deep
Big and bushy just like sheep.

There is a dark brown monkey
It looks and sounds very funky.

The volcano is blowing with deadly force
The horse is running around the course.

The clouds are pink
Like coloured ink.

Naomi Payne (8)
Riverview Junior School

Summer Days!

Paddling pools
Burning sun
People out
Having fun.

Sweaty foreheads
Hot hands
Boiling back
In the sands.

The blue carpet
In your reach
You go across
The sandy beach.

You jump in
It's really cold
You keep swimming
Being bold.

Out you get
You're going home
Once you're there
You're on the phone.

Paddling pool
Burning sun
People out
Having fun!

Amy Fisher (11)
St Paulinus CE Primary School, Crayford

Old Photos

'Who's that?'
'Uncle Jim.'
'What's he doing?'
'Drinking gin.'

'Who's that?'
'Aunt Mary.'
'What's she doing?'
'Making people less hairy.'

'Who's that?'
'My friend Chris.'
'What's he doing?'
'Giving you a kiss.'

'Who's that?'
'David Beckham.'
'What's he doing?'
'Driving to Peckham.

'Who's that?'
'Your cousin Joe.'
'What's he doing?'
'Chasing a crow.'

'Who's that?'
'That's you Billy.'
'What am I doing?'
'Being silly.'

Scott Mitchell & Chris Lees (11)
St Paulinus CE Primary School, Crayford

My Family

My family is a big family,
With my mum with one sister,
And my dad with six sisters.

I have lots of cousins
And aunties and uncles,
Grandads and grandmas
And their brothers and sisters too.

I've got loads of cousins
From every age,
I've got two that live near me
And go to my school.

First there's Matthew,
Then there's Luke,
One is seven,
One is four,
Living together every day,
Sometimes I even go round to play.

Then there's all my other cousins,
Too many to describe,
Now I'm going to have to leave you
With the story of my life.

James Mason (10)
St Paulinus CE Primary School, Crayford

Summertime

In the summertime when the weather is fine
All the kids queue up in a line
Jump into the paddling pool which I'm glad to say is mine
The cold drinks are coming quick and fast
Don't get out of the queue kids, or you will be last.

Leah Jeffery (11)
St Paulinus CE Primary School, Crayford

The Spooky House

Outside the spooky house,
You could not hear a single mouse,
But when you opened the rotting door,
You would know this place was haunted for sure!

As soon as you walked up the creaky stairs,
I think you will find you are in for a scare,
There were pictures of spooky-looking people on the wall,
Not a cosy feeling at all!

There was a cold feeling in the air,
And I shouted, 'Is there anybody there?'
But no one answered so I guessed I was alone,
And in the distance I heard a hungry groan!

Where could I go to? Where could I hide,
Before this thing found me and ate me alive!
I found myself running as fast as I could
I think I was running like no ordinary man.

I entered a room and I sat very still,
I could feel my heart beating, I felt ever so ill,
Should I stay here or should I go?
The choice was mine but I just did not know!

The choice was not mine for in walked this 'thing'
It was big, fat and hairy without any skin,
It had three crooked eyes and a misshapen nose,
Would it let me go now? No I don't suppose.

It gobbled me up without any hitch,
I kept falling and falling into his bottomless pit,
I waited and waited what could I say?
This really had been a truly terrible day.

Liam Smith (11)
St Paulinus CE Primary School, Crayford

Who's That

'Who's that?'
'That's Gran.'
'Doing what?'
'Getting a frying pan.'

'Who's that?'
'That's Jim,'
'Doing what?'
'Drinking gin.'

'Who's that?'
'That's Pip,'
'Doing what?'
'Biting her lip.'

'Who's that?'
'That's Pa-Pa,'
'Doing what?'
'Singing da da.'

Robert Elliott (11)
St Paulinus CE Primary School, Crayford

The One That Got Away!

Sitting on the bank watching mist rise,
The water so still under blue skies,
Like a shimmering blanket over a bed,
Relaxing, no worries circling round in my head.
My bait in the box, I watch them squirm,
Most of them maggots, some of them worms,
My keepnet is ready, waiting for the catch,
I can't wait to see the biggest of the batch.
I hold my rod tight and the reel starts to spin,
The strength of the fish nearly pulling me in,
It's massive, it's huge, wow! what a day,
Oh dear!
They will never believe the one that got away.

Callum Togwell (11)
St Paulinus CE Primary School, Crayford

Muddled Up Magic

Right, I think I've got it . . .

One eye of frog,
Toe of newt,
Ear of hog,
Makes me . . . puke!

Maybe not, let's try . . .

Bladder of pig,
Leg of roach,
Bits of twig,
Makes me . . . choke!

This has got to work . . .

Tongue of wolf,
A drop of rum,
Mushy chalk,
Makes me . . . gone?

Sophie Kingston (10)
St Paulinus CE Primary School, Crayford

Postponed

The rain pours down and drenches us but never dims
The passion.
The snow falls and engulfs us as if it's going out of fashion.
But the crowds regardless, to cheer on their team,
Despite the pelt of hailstones,
The biggest ever seen.

And then, with just an hour to go,
As we stand, iced to the bone,
The man on the tannoy tells us
That the game has been postponed!

Jack Phillips (10)
St Paulinus CE Primary School, Crayford

A Teacher's Life For Me

I argue and I reason,
I preach and you will learn.
I understand you're suffering,
Your freedom, I know you yearn.

For years I trained to help you,
Your futures are in my hands.
Your only fun is playtime,
The rest of the time is bland.

Open those books and pick up your pens,
It's time for the lesson now to begin.
I'll guide you and teach you so listen with care,
My knowledge of the world I'll gladly share.

I'll mark your work with judgement,
With emphasis on perfection.
Exemplary work will be acknowledged,
Poor efforts will only bring a grade of rejection.

Your minds I will guide and nurture,
We'll work as a team for sure.
School life is only a prelude,
To a lifetime of learning more.

It excites me when you grasp a concept,
Of a task we set before, unknown.
With my guidance and encouragement,
Because I've done my job, your intelligence has now grown.

For me to help you through these years,
Hard times we will experience, but we will progress.
It brings me joy and happiness,
To see you finally with good grades, good health and good
Success!

Samuel Stone (11)
St Paulinus CE Primary School, Crayford

Who's That?

'Who's that?'
'That's Auntie Mable,'
'What's she doing?'
'Cleaning out the stable.'

'Who's that?'
'Your uncle Alex.'
'What's he doing?'
'Walking in the annex.'

'Who's that?'
'My sister Sally.'
'What's she doing?'
'Walking in the valley.'

'Who's that?'
'Fat Fred.'
'What is he doing?'
'Going to bed.'

'Who's that?'
'Callum the cat.'
'What's he doing?'
'Being hit by a bat.'

'Who's that?'
'You.'
'What am I doing?'
'Counting to two.'

'Who's that?'
'Dave the dog.'
'What's he doing?'
'Chasing a frog.'

Jack Sharp (11)
St Paulinus CE Primary School, Crayford

The Seasons

Winter is a cold and dark season,
The nights are long and the days are short.
The trees are bare and their leaves are scattered across the ground,
In the morning an icy frost covers the ground.
The next season is spring,
The air is crisp and fresh.
Buds are growing on the plants,
Showers help things to bloom and grow.
When summer comes everything is fully grown,
The days are long and the nights are short.
The air is warm and it smells of flowers,
Bees hover over flowers to collect nectar.
When the leaves start to fade and drop you know autumn is coming,
Leaves fall to the ground and crunch under our feet.
Everything is red and brown like the conkers on the ground,
As the nights get longer you know that winter is coming.

Max Fountain (10)
St Paulinus CE Primary School, Crayford

Winter

He throws the miserable clouds across the sky,
As he sprays his shower of water upon us.

The sky darkens as he goes to sleep,
And the night is quiet for everyone.

He throws his spears which bang and clash
across the sky.

We pray for sun as his terrible reign comes
to an end.

He struggles to fight the sun.
As his power is not strong enough.

The almighty sun defeats him,
In this long war.

George Bartholomew (11)
St Paulinus CE Primary School, Crayford

At The Beach

Splashing water
getting wet
Swimming with new friends
that you met

Happy families
having fun
Getting brown
in the sun.

Being at the beach
is such a joy
It is a feeling that
we must enjoy.

Little shade
burning back
Lying on a
lilo flat.

Sweaty foreheads
cool sundaes
Laughing children
in the rays.

Suhanya Jeyashiri (11)
St Paulinus CE Primary School, Crayford

Sunny Days

Bright and sunny days are cool,
The trees and flowers are beautiful
Children playing in the pool,
Big children, little children, any size at all,
Everybody wants a tan,
But everyone's frying like a chip pan.
Ice creams melting in the sun,
Everybody's having fun.

Hollie Brown (11)
St Paulinus CE Primary School, Crayford

Fire! Fire!

Fire! Fire! burning the door,
Fire! Fire! on the floor.
Fire! Fire! on my bed,
Fire! Fire! don't I dread.

Fire! Fire! up the wall,
Fire! Fire! scares us all.
Fire! Fire! bullying my ted,
Fire! Fire! yellow, orange and red.

Fire! Fire! small and tall,
Fire! Fire! in the hall.
Fire! Fire! on my clothes,
Fire! Fire! on our toes.

Fire! Fire! moving fast,
Fire! Fire! let's run past.
Fire! Fire! near the TV
Fire! Fire! hurting me.

Water! Water! turn it on
Water! Water! fire's gone.
Water! Water! turn it off,
Smoke! Smoke! still making us cough.

Samantha Selby (10)
St Paulinus CE Primary School, Crayford

Who?

I like to run around and play,
To jump up and down and catch my prey.
I live in the wild and I have black and orange stripes,
And like to jump from very big heights.
I have sharp claws and beady brown eyes,
And crouch down low as if me and my friends are spies.

Who am I . . . ?

Jessica Board (11)
St Paulinus CE Primary School, Crayford

Twilight

No moon, no sun,
No guardian of the sky.
Keep your eyes shut or otherwise
Who knows what you might spy?
Light has fallen, darkness will reign,
Like in the battles of old,
The wind is howling, wailing, screaming,
The air is blood-chillingly cold.
That's not the sky, it's purple smoke,
Wafting out from a witch's pot,
The stars are sparks from a wizard's staff,
Whether you know so or not.
Listen to me, I tell you this,
Midnight is not the time to fear,
For twilight is when the shadows are long
And the evil ones are near.
But this time will end so very soon,
When the moon rises in the sky,
For once more a gentle, kind leader,
Sits on her throne up high.

Lauren Blood (11)
St Paulinus CE Primary School, Crayford

Witches

Down in the woods where the trees are bare,
And twigs scritch-scratch to rip your hair,
There in the light of the silver moon
Blue-haired witches sit and croon
In flowing capes and pointed hats,
Around a cauldron filled with bats.
They fly on broomsticks way up high,
To sweep dark cobwebs from the sky . . .
These blue-haired, red-eyed witches.

Abbie Noakes (10)
St Paulinus CE Primary School, Crayford

Minotor, Minotaur

Minotaur, Minotaur, tell me why
Why did you kill and terrify
All those young people who came to try
To keep their lives and not to die!

I didn't mean it, it was a mistake
I held out my paw to give a handshake
But as I did they began to quake
I'm not like that for goodness sake.

Minotaur, Minotaur didn't you know
Those quivering people expected aggro?
Your popularity was below zero
You were just meant to live solo.

I thought they wanted to be my friend
Until I came to a horrible end
All I ask is remember me
Remember me, remember me!

Alexandra Kerr (11)
St Paulinus CE Primary School, Crayford

My Cat

Soft and fluffy is my cat's fur,
And all the time she likes to purr.
She likes to play with my nan's ball of wool
Or my sister's bouncy ball.

She wags her tail when she has a dream,
And when she's awake licks my ice cream
She's very pretty her name is Molly
And she has a twin sister called Holly.

Holly Board (11)
St Paulinus CE Primary School, Crayford

Old Photographs

'Who's that?'
'That's Auntie Jane.'
'What's she doing?'
'Being a pain.'

'Who's that?'
'That's Uncle Fred.'
'What's he doing?'
'Going to bed.'

'Who's that?'
'That's Auntie Kerry.'
'What's she doing?'
'Drinking sherry.'

'Who's that?'
'That's Uncle Bill.'
'What's he doing?'
'Taking a pill.'

'Who's that?'
'That's me.'
'What are you doing?'
'Climbing a tree.'

'Who's that?'
'That's you.'
'What am I doing?'
'Going to the loo.'

Glen Chute (10)
St Paulinus CE Primary School, Crayford

Why Not?

'Can I have a snack Mum?'
'No.'
'Why not?'
'Because you can't, alright!'

'Dad can I have a snack?'
'No!'
'Why not?'
'Stop bugging me and go away!'
'You always let my brother have one
And you always let my sister have one
So what's the matter with me?'

'Mum can I have a snack?'
'No?'
'Why not?'
'Because you have just had your lunch alright,
now stop pestering me and go and have a drink.'
'No, because I don't want a drink, I want a snack.
If you give me a snack then I'll stop pestering you!'
'Fine, go and have a snack.'

'Oh no!'
'What?'
'They're all gone.'

Jasmine Stacey (10)
St Paulinus CE Primary School, Crayford

Dreams

Waves of silver, crimson and cream
Sparkling like a sunlit stream
Drops of silver, jets of joy
Reflecting like a cheerful boy.
Golden ripples,
Frosty glimmer upon your face
It's a dreamy, unreal place.

Kieron Merritt (11)
Saxon Way Primary School

Silly Little Rhymes

Of all the things that are in the world,
Rhymes are the favourite,
Some of them make your skin crawl
And some have disgusting bits.
If you were to write a recipe,
On how to bake a cake,
Wouldn't it be a lot more fun
If a silly little rhyme you'd make?

A silly little rhyme it can,
Cheer up any sad soul,
It brings laughter, joy and happiness,
So really on the whole,
If you were going for a walk,
Down beside a lake,
Wouldn't it be a lot more fun
If a silly little rhyme you'd make?

Writing rhymes can be good,
For any person's heart,
Then reading it afterwards,
That's the really good part.
So when you are going out,
To give the leaves a rake,
Wouldn't it be a lot more fun
If a silly little rhyme you'd make?

Lauren Weeks (10)
Saxon Way Primary School

Bobin And Robin

There was a young foal called Bobin
Who had a mate called Robin
All day they played and ran a long way
By the end of the day their feet were throbbing
The foal fell over and he was sobbing.

Rhianne Lowe (8)
Saxon Way Primary School

The Stream

The stream is running down the road
Like a pea pod on a lorry load.
The stream is sparkling like a butterfly
Dashing and darting by.
The stream is beautiful, calm and kind,
Just carry on flowing and flowing by.
The stream is twinkling like a star
Very brightly almost nightly.
The stream is friendly, like a cheerful girl
Graceful as a twisting whirl.
The stream is colourful and clean,
You see right through it like a dream.

Suann Brignall (11)
Saxon Way Primary School

Bumblebee

Bumblebee, bumblebee sitting in the tree
Why are you waiting, waiting for me?

You could have gone sailing or flown round the tree,
Bumblebee, bumblebee don't wait for me.

If you see people passing by
Don't say hello, just say goodbye.
Bumblebee, bumblebee stay in that tree,
Don't you come back, waiting for me.

Bumblebee, bumblebee, you now have to go
But tell me one thing that I ought to know.
Why do you sing your happy song all . . . day long?
Bye-bye bumblebee, don't be long.

Abbygail Isitt-Lee (10)
Saxon Way Primary School

Animal Poem

Fish swim, birds fly,
Deep water, blue sky.

Cats miaow, dogs bark,
Comfy cushion, kennel dark.

Dolphins splash, whales blow
Underwater, down below.

Rabbits burrow, guinea pigs squeak,
Amongst the carrots, take a peek.

Horses gallop, tortoise slow,
Along the meadow, let them go.

Hamsters nibble, mice do too,
Tasty treats, in my zoo!

Claire Goldsmith (8)
Saxon Way Primary School

Wander

Wander Witch went wandering on a cold and frosty night.
She saw a wizard in a garden and she gave him such a fright.
The wizard cast a spell that caught our Wander Witch
Who flew up in the air then fell into a ditch.
As she got up she screamed loud and clearly,
'You evil wizard you'll play for this dearly!
Huff and puff, kick you too, I cast this evil wicked spell on you.'

Becky Bedwell (11)
Saxon Way Primary School

Seasons

Autumn
The colour of autumn is gold,
And the crops from the farms have been sold,
The gifts for the harvest,
From smallest to largest,
Are a wonderful sight to behold.

Winter
In winter we suffer the snows,
The wind just blows and blows,
Down comes the rain,
Oh! we're all soaked again,
And I've only just dried out my toes.

Spring
The clocks go forward in spring,
All the birds in the morning they sing,
They drive us all mad,
Especially my dad,
Who cannot abide such a thing.

Summer
In summer we lie in the sun,
Just sitting around having fun,
Sometimes it's too hot,
To run round a lot,
We're glad that all our work's done.

Bethan Evans (9)
Sheldwich Primary School

Elli

There once was a young girl called Elli,
Who always watched The Simpsons on telly,
She watched it so much,
Her brain got mucked up,
Oh that silly young girl called Elli.

Emmeline Kerkvliet (11)
Sheldwich Primary School

Snow Christmas Song

Snow
The snow is falling
The air is calling
Make a snowman
As you see the postman.

Christmas
Christmas has gone now
Decorations are down
Celebrate New Year
Birthdays are near.

Songs
You're singing a song
And dancing along
You're at a party
Eating smarties.

Emma Godden (9)
Sheldwich Primary School

Cats

There once was a cat called Soks,
Who always had chickenpox,
She stuck her claws up her nose,
Not forgetting the toes,
Then needed a detox!

There once was a cat called Izzy,
Who was always very busy,
He caught lots of mice,
Then cooked them in rice,
Then he ate them fizzy!

There once was a cat called Tigi,
Who liked to do the jiggy,
She danced all day,
She had no time to play,
So she ate and became a piggy!

Livvy Corke (10)
Sheldwich Primary School

The Secret Concert

We walk into the concert hall
waiting to see who's coming on
it was Busted my favourite band
I hoped they'd ask me to sing along.

The crowd was screaming
waving their hands
I joined in too and
sang with the band.

The music thumping through my ear
like people beating drums.
I like them using their guitars
strumming them with their thumbs.

Busted sing as loud as can be
I've never heard them sing before
we're stamping and screaming
and jumping on the floor.

The show is nearly over
we've got to say goodbye
I go to get their autograph
I can't get to them, even if I try and try.

Alice Maw (10)
Sheldwich Primary School

Untitled

I once knew an ugly fellow
I think he was an Orc
I asked him if he liked his job
But he could barely talk.

There once was an elf
Who liked to put up shelves
He went to put some up one day
But on the wall they would not stay.

Rory Higgins (9)
Sheldwich Primary School

School

I get up in the morning at 7 o'clock
I lock the door at 8 o'clock
At 9 o'clock school has started
At 10 o'clock it's maths once again
At 11 o'clock it's time for fun
Because break has started, time to run
At 12 o'clock time for science
Experiments, more fun
At 1 o'clock I'm hungry again, that's OK it's lunchtime
At 2 o'clock it's literacy, time to learn some words
At 3 o'clock it's home time, hooray
No more work until another day
At 4 o'clock this time I am starving
Roast potatoes and peas, yum-yum
At 8 o'clock I am very tired, let's go to bed

Hello! It's another day, ready for school again.

James Wilson (9)
Sheldwich Primary School

At Midnight When The Moon Is Bright

At midnight when the moon is bright
There roams a creature filled with might
With eyes like glinting candlelight.

Its yellow teeth like deadly spears
Bring back ghosts of your worst fears
There comes a rustle only she hears.

Your mistake is a sign to her
She unfurls limbs all covered in fur
And still you do not even stir.

And up she jumps and gives a purr.

Leila Pain (9)
Sheldwich Primary School

Golden Eagle

I saw a golden eagle,
perched sadly on a branch.
Eating nothing but rotten leaves
a freezing day in March.

He never came to eat the meat
for fear of being hurt.
His keeper stood with pole and chain
with a skull on his howlett's shirt.

I want to see him happy
set him free if I could.
But this is how my story ends
perched on a piece of wood.

Shannon Regan-Dunn (10)
Sheldwich Primary School

Spring

The thing I like about the spring
Is the fresh air that it will bring,
I love being outside when the sun shines,
the dappled sunlight under the pines.

The ducklings are swimming, they've left the nest,
Their winter coats gone, now they're finally dressed,
The farmers are in their fields to sow the plants
that will go to grow and grow.

The grass in the meadow pops up all over
Filled with poppies and flowers and clover
In those meadows are piglets and lambs
That turn in the autumn into chops and hams.

Emily Hammond (9)
Sheldwich Primary School

The Seasons

When spring arrives it makes me cheery
the flowers spring up and
I feel less dreary.

As weeks roll on
and days get warmer,
it must be nearly time for summer.
So we go and play outside.

In autumn it starts to get colder,
we start to put on our hats
and scarves.

In wintertime it's really dreary,
when the sun doesn't shine
it makes me weary.

Tilly Manning (9)
Sheldwich Primary School

My School

Child bringer,
Aching finger,
Excessive learning,
Brain burning,
Dinner hall,
Bouncing ball,
Sport races,
Tying laces,
Stressed teacher,
A bad feature,
Broke a rule,
Banned from school!

Charles Dixon (11)
Sheldwich Primary School

My Special Friend

I have this very special friend
I talk to him every day
He never seems to mind a bit
And just listens anyway.

He is such a special friend
I love him very much
We like to share a daily cuddle
Then I pop him in his hutch!

Rachael Welch (10)
Sheldwich Primary School

The Wolf! Cinquain

The wolf!
Eyes of fury,
The bayer to the moon,
He's the one who cannot be tamed,
The wolf!

Katherine Gauld (11)
Sheldwich Primary School

School

Hymn in the hall
Educational,
Playing games,
Reaching aims,
Brain burning,
Excessive learning,
Having lunch,
Hanging in a bunch,
Playing with a ball,
At my school.

Lauren Hennessy (10)
Sheldwich Primary School

I Feel Ill

Coughing and sneezing,
Snoring and wheezing

Painful headaches and
Hurtful tummy aches

I really feel ill,
Is it a chill?

Someone believe me,
I really feel ill!

Samantha Cook (11)
Sheldwich Primary School

A Rock

Shin whacker
Elbow smacker
Thigh splitter
Blood dripper
Groin acher
Hole maker.

Dominic Mulford (10)
Sheldwich Primary School

There Once Was A Boy Called Duke

There once was a boy called Duke
When I looked at him he made me puke
So I put on dark glasses,
And hid in the grasses,
And hoped it was only a fluke.

Matthew Hewson (10)
Sheldwich Primary School

From A Hot Air Balloon

As I set off from the ground
I see the Earth going round and round
The things below gradually get smaller
As I climb up taller and taller
Now I'm up in the air
Tiny people stop and stare
Then I slowly float down
Heading towards the little town.

Rebecca Smith (11)
The Brent Primary School

Snow Is Falling

The early morning glow
Shines through the falling snow
The whistling of the gentle breeze
Blows through the snowy trees.
Everything white as far as I can see
Not a sound
Not even the buzzing of a bumblebee.

Beth Johnson (8)
The Brent Primary School

Love Is Pink

Love is pink
It tastes like strawberry bubblegum,
and smells like fresh red roses.
It's like a big pink heart
and sounds like two doves twooing,
It feels like you've been shot in the heart!

April Fenge (10)
The Brent Primary School

The Witch's Spell

Round about the cauldron go,
In the cat's crunchy head we throw.
Rabbit's ears chopped off fresh
A bit of human's bloody flesh.
Next we throw some frizzy hair,
Then a furry ear of a bear.

Double, double toil and trouble
Fire burn and cauldron bubble.

In we throw two human's crunchy eyes
Next watch out two apple pies.
Now a gerbil's rotten feet,
Then a piece of hard cow's meat.

Double, double toil and trouble
Fire burn and cauldron bubble!

Rebeka Balloch (10)
The Brent Primary School

Dear Cat

Thank you for the invitation
To your cosy dinner for two,
I'd really love to come
But I've got the flu.
I'm sure it would be lovely
To dine with you this day
But to be honest with you
I have to say,
You're ugly, you're a mean old cat,
You're sick, and you're ever so fat.

Yours sincerely
Mouse.

Hannah Bradley (10)
The Brent Primary School

From A Hot Air Balloon

We are in a hot air balloon and we're getting high,
Everything is getting smaller every time
We're getting taller as the world is getting smaller,
As we're looking down it is getting cooler
Then the cars turn smaller.

Everywhere we go we may see the world
In our hot air balloon,
It is a model world,
It's very cold up here so let's go and see
Some beautiful sights,
The world is very small up here so let's go nearer to land.

Now we're going to land,
So say goodbye, so bye bye bye.

Demi Joy (10)
The Brent Primary School

The Magic Box

(Based on 'Magic Box' by Kit Wright)

I will put in the box . . .
The splash of swimming in the shivering
cold sea.

I will put in the box . . .
Freezing fresh coke floating and fizzing
in your mouth.
Melty, marshy, mouth-watering marshmallows.

I will put in the box . . .
A flying candy car throwing candy out the window.
Teacher with a microphone and a singer with children.
Fireman and a police car
And a policeman with a fire engine.

Jade Cruttenden (10)
The Brent Primary School

Fear

Fear is black
With the taste of dark liquorice
And the smell of smoke in a fire
It sounds like a fire-breathing dragon
Fear feels like a dark tunnel and you never
Know where you are going.

George Reynolds (10)
The Brent Primary School

From A Hot Air Balloon

Slower than the worm going up and up
I see the sea as the balloon grows
I see the town glitter as the sun bounces off the car roofs.

From here the white fluffy clouds break as I slither through them
I can see the world beneath my feet
The buildings and people look like Playmobile
And the signs look like lollipops
I'm lowering to the ground, so that view has disappeared.

Jake Turner (10)
The Brent Primary School

Happiness

Happiness is yellow and bright as the sunshine.
It tastes like candy and sweets,
It smells like fresh roses just come from the shop,
It looks like sunset on the top of the ocean,
It sounds like singing happy birthday on the radio,
It feels like the softness of my fur coat.

Natalie Day (9)
The Brent Primary School

The Magic Box
(Based on 'Magic Box' by Kit Wright)

I will put in the box . . .
A sparkling star from the summer sky,
A fire fish from the floor of the foggy sea
And the sound of the topsy turvy waves.

Hannah Chapman (10)
The Brent Primary School

Happiness

Happiness is the light yellow,
The taste of a chocolate bar.
Happiness smells like roses,
Happiness looks like the sunshine,
Happiness sounds like laughter,
It felt like a comfortable bed.

Oliver Symmons (10)
The Brent Primary School

Laziness

Laziness is black,
It lasts like bitter lemon,
It smells like dirty washing,
It looks like a pigsty,
It sounds boring,
It feels weird.

Sam Allen (9)
The Brent Primary School

Snowman

S now creatures, snowmen, snow ladies and snow hens
N one of them last in the sun, so next year you make another one
O n a day when there's snow, people with sledges are on the go
W inter days are as cold as ice, anyway it's still nice
M ost people make snowmen, but some might make snow den
A nybody who trashes snowmen will go in, who'll be laughing then?
N obody ever hates the snow, especially Santa, ho-ho-ho.

Reece Doyle (10)
The Brent Primary School

The Magic Box

(Based on 'Magic Box' by Kit Wright)

I will put in the box . . .
A twist of a tough, a tug of a tooth,
A melting mole, a mangled magazine.
The breath of a dragon, a flame of a fire,
A dog with a miaow, a cat with a bark,
A lion with a long neck, a giraffe with a mane,
A dog with good breath, a man with dog's breath.

Carlie Niyazi (10)
The Brent Primary School

Sadness

Sadness is blue
The taste of plain water
Smells like tears running down my face
It looks like an empty box
Sadness sounds like a sad song
Sadness feels like a rough surface.

Grace Potthurst (10)
The Brent Primary School

The Magic Box

(Based on 'Magic Box' by Kit Wright)

I will put in the box . . .
Spinning spiders on a silky web
A wing of a griffin that flew across the sky.

I will put in the box . . .
A policeman with a microphone
A singer with a police car.

I will put in the box . . .
A sailor with a van
A witch with a football
A boy with spells
A cat with a gun
A hunter with claws.

Kimberly Smail (10)
The Brent Primary School

Once Upon A Time Machine

Once upon a time machine,
I woke up in a creep scene,
The queen was only sixteen
The king was made of margarine.
A jelly bean stole my TV screen
My mum's hair was covered in cream
Once upon a time machine.

Once upon a time machine
My dog went bright green,
I was made of ice cream,
I had a really scary dream,
Once upon a time machine.

Nicole Sherwood (10)
The Brent Primary School

Happiness

Happiness is a sunny yellow.
It tastes like freshly made bread in the morning.
It smells like freshly cut flowers.
It looks like butterflies.
It sounds joyful and it feels like home.

Rebecca Newnham (10)
The Brent Primary School

Once Upon A Time Machine

Once upon a time machine
I woke up in the cricket team,
The crazy theme was hot ice cream,
All the animals had turned bright green,
The king and queen suddenly turned mean,
Once upon a time machine.

Richard Blows (10)
The Brent Primary School

Fear

Fear is ghostly white,
It tastes like bitter wind.
It smells like a chilly winter's day.
It looks like a see-through ghost.
It sounds like the rustling of leaves in the park.
Fear feels like a ghost going right through you.

Christopher Slater (10)
The Brent Primary School

Enigma's Confusion

Confusion is a dark black
It tastes like bitter coffee
It smells like a wave of different aromas
And it looks like a giant spiral
It sounds like air
It feels like you're upside down on a roller coaster.

Jordan Morley (10)
The Brent Primary School

Magic Box

(Based on 'Magic Box' by Kit Wright)

I will put in the box . . .
Flaming fish in a frying pan
A tree that is a purple-blue and green.

I will put in the box . . .
A cloud
A wizard doing the splits
A singer with a wand
And a wizard with a microphone.

Courtney Merrick (9)
The Brent Primary School

Happiness

Happiness is red
It tastes like candyfloss
It smells like flowers
It looks like a day that's been snowing
It sounds like people laughing in the park
It feels like you have won a million pounds.

Ben Santinella (9)
The Brent Primary School

Dear Shark

Thank you for your invitation
I'd really love to come
But I've had a better offer
From somebody quite glum
Her name is Sally Seal
And she has recently been ill!
I really need to see her
To give her the magic pill.
I'm very, very sorry
I'd really love to come
She wants me to be there
And me and you weren't the best of friends.

Yours sincerely
Fish.

Shannon Homden (10)
The Brent Primary School

Dodger At The Contest

Dodger's waggy tail,
And his fur so furry,
Black and white it cannot fail,
And his sweet little pawprints, so dirty.

Floppy ears,
And his sweet smile,
If he doesn't win, there will be some tears,
We're going to find out in a while.

You're going to get food when we get home, a whole tin!
And all of his brill tricks,
It's a win,
I know you're excited, please don't lick.

Deena Braxton (9)
The Brent Primary School

Sadness

Sadness is black
It tastes like sloshy peaches
It smells like a sweaty T-shirt
It looks like rain falling from the sky
It sounds like a kitten crying
It feels like losing in the Cup Final.

Coy Hardy (10)
The Brent Primary School

What Can It Be?

Fast runner
Show jumper
Four legs
Big feet
Hay eater
Stubborn thing
Rearing forward
Bucking backwards
Tail swinger
What can it be?

A horse.

Ellicia Roberts (9)
The Brent Primary School

Happiness

Happiness is light blue
It tastes like cold tea
It smells like fresh doughnuts
It sounds like circle round toast
It feels like glass smashing.

Harvinder Rai (10)
The Brent Primary School

Snow

It crunches when you walk on it
It falls down whirling gently
It is as cold as ice
It sparkles as if glitter has been sprinkled on it
Yes it is snow.

Ryan Cherry (9)
The Brent Primary School

Sweet Little Butterfly

A sweet little butterfly flying through the air
Its lovely, colourful pink and purple wings are bare.
Why should they be bare at this time of year?
Although for this time of year it's quite clear.
Maybe she's going to a hot place
Where she might find a different face.
But I wonder, has she got a suitcase?
Because it's going to be a long ride
So when she gets there hopefully she'll be full of pride.

Kirstie Weeks (9)
The Brent Primary School

Shooting Star

Shooting star goes across the sky,
Lighting up the world as it does fly.
Passing by the big, huge world,
Not one cry heard.
Shooting star your work is done,
Goodbye shooting star, you're number one.

Charlotte Wickens (9)
The Brent Primary School

The Spider And The Snake Dinner Party

Dear Spider

Thank you for your invitation
for your cosy dinner for two
I would really like to come
But I really don't know what to do
I will let you know
I will wear my red bow
So I hope you can come
My old funny chum
I'm waiting for you
Mrs Sindylou

Yours sincerely
Mr Snake.

Danielle Findlay (10)
The Brent Primary School

Sleek Shark

His sharp teeth,
His crooked smile,
Not one like a crocodile.
His wide head,
His long tail,
His tall fin like a sail.
His diving tricks,
His slobbery licks,
Not pleasant I'm sure,
He's a fast swimmer,
Do look out,
You never know,
Whether you're his favourite chew.

Kelly Haines (10)
The Brent Primary School

Christmas Poems

Christmas

C runchy white snow to freeze the snowmen
H ot chocolate for when you come in from building your models
R ichly made presents by Santa Claus' elves
I cy garden lawns with the pond frozen
S uper veg with gravy
T errific Christmas dinner with crunchy roast potatoes
M asses of presents under the tree
A mazing gleaming lights on every tree's a treat
S kating on the ice pond.

Snowman

S now is great in the cold!
N o one hates the snow
O n Thursday we made snow creatures
W hat a day it was, what a day
M ad people made snow angels
A warding the best snow creature
N oses look like Rudolph.

Scott Rudd (8)
The Brent Primary School

Snow

Look at sparkling frosty snow
Whirling down to the ground.

White and crispy, light and soft
Icy white snow.

Hanging icicles just waiting to melt
Children making snowballs.
So come on snow, snow a little more
For all to enjoy.

Emma Hannay (9)
The Brent Primary School

What Is Violet?

What is red?
A rose is red
Smells so lovely and fine.

What is blue?
The sky is blue
Filled with puffy white clouds.

What is green?
The grass is green
It sways in the blowing wind.

What is yellow?
A sunset is yellow
And it beams in the sky.

What is pink?
A piglet is pink
That lays asleep in hay.

What is orange?
A tiger is orange
Looks as sweet as a toy.

What is violet?
A violet is violet
Looks like a simple violet.

Leah Shine (10)
The Brent Primary School

Snow!

Snow is like a whirling cloud falling from the sky
Snow is great, it's fluffy, it is icy.
Snow is like a soft clump of cotton wool,
Snow is like a soft gentle swan swimming peacefully in a lake,
Ice makes you slip and slide,
Snow is like a great hundred thousand doves attacking,
Snow is like a soft carpet.

Oliver Willbye (9)
The Brent Primary School

Christmas

C hildren play with white sparkly snow
H appy people put Christmas decorations up
R ed roses start to appear at snowtime
I n the house you can smell aroma of a turkey
S lippers are being worn round the house to keep feet warm
T rees are getting decorated all over the world
M erry people sing Christmas carols
A ll the people have a great day opening presents
S aucy turkey gets eaten.

Natasha Nash (9)
The Brent Primary School

Dolphin

Dolphins are kind, gentle and sweet
All put together it makes a big treat.
Not only that, they're shiny and blue
And you'll like them too.

Charlotte Roffey (10)
The Brent Primary School

Christmas Poem

C hildren are singing their Christmas songs,
H olly on the Christmas table,
R ed cheeks from the winter's frost,
I cy roads that cars skid on,
S now is falling everywhere,
T oys are wrapped for Christmas day,
'M erry Christmas,' the people say,
A very happy time of year,
S anta comes every year to give us presents that we enjoy.

Rebecca Letchford (9)
The Brent Primary School

Snowflake

S ee the snow patting against the window,
N oses red like Rudolph's,
O ld, soft, fluffy, white snow,
W hite, melting snow,
F alling, touching snow,
L ovely children in the snow,
A ll the choirs outside, singing,
K icking through the crunchy, white snow,
E veryone enjoys making snowmen and snow angels.

Abbie Hales (9)
The Brent Primary School

Dolphin

Dark blue, light grey
Swishy tail
Past the sail
Lay in the seabed
As if they're lead
Smooth skin,
Bumpy fin.

Megan Pearson (10)
The Brent Primary School

Christmas

C runchy white snow to play with
H ot turkey for Christmas dinner
R ed robins chirp their Christmas song in the snowy air,
I cy gardens where it's been snowing
S parkly snow falls to the ground
T errific Christmas pudding
M um cooks deliciously
A unty Deb gives me amazing presents
S hivering in the cold.

Joseph Reynolds (8)
The Brent Primary School

Silver Star

I wish I was a silver star
In the sky at night
Sparkling through the darkness
With my little light
Sparkling in the night-time
But never in the day
It's only when you go to bed
That I come out to play.

Josh Heaton (9)
The Brent Primary School

What Can It Be?

Long-legged
Big-headed
Run while
Smashed tile
Loud jumper
Winter's wonder
What can it be?

Daisy Walker (9)
The Brent Primary School

Christmas Poem

C hristmas lights twinkling brightly
H appy holly trees thriving out in the woods
R uby-red robins chirp their merry winter song
 I make crystal-white snowmen in the cold morning air,
S now clutches at the branches of swaying trees,
T rees rock to and fro creaking as they go
M any years since long ago we still know the story of Jesus
A lthough Christmas happens once a year joy is everywhere
S anta's reindeer soar through the sky, not making a sound
   as they fly.

Mireille Patrick (9)
The Brent Primary School

Christmas

C arols are lovely
H omes have good decorations
R eindeers pull the sleigh
I cicles hanging from homes
S anta eats mince pies
T oys are made at Santa's workshop
M any people sing carols
A ntlers on reindeers
S anta goes, 'Ho! Ho! Ho! Ho! Ho! Ho! Ho!'

Joshua Jarvis (9)
The Brent Primary School

Happiness

Happiness is bright yellow
and tastes like ice cream melting on your tongue
and smells like fresh red roses in a vase.
Happiness looks like children splashing in a swimming pool
and sounds like children's laughter spreading in the air.
Happiness feels like the best thing you could want.

Emma McCartney (10)
The Brent Primary School

Christmas

C alendars are great
H omes are brilliantly decorated
R eindeers are very strong and fast
I ce is freezing cold
S un is most likely to not come out at winter
T oys are superb
M any people like Christmas
A ntlers can't break easily
S anta goes, 'Ho! Ho! Ho!'

Jonathan May (8)
The Brent Primary School

Dear Fox

Dear Fox

Thank you for your invitation
to your cosy dinner for two,
I'd really love to come,
But I can't think what to do.
I need to go and see my grandad,
As he has brought me a pair of shoes,
I'm sure it would be a blast,
But at the minute I have the blues.
I don't see the point of coming all that way,
Could I come round,
One other day?

Yours sincerely
Rabbit

Lauren Dixon (11)
The Brent Primary School

From A Hot-Air Balloon

Up, up and away
I'm getting higher and higher, things smaller and smaller,
We're drifting away, it's getting colder and colder
I've got a lovely view, it's absolutely beautiful.

I can see a long dirty river with huge meanders that look like snakes
They look like beetles scurrying along but they're cars.

As I get higher, I get colder and colder
There are shiny fields that reflect from the sun.

We're coming down now it's a lot warmer
Things are getting bigger
The balloon has landed, the journey is over.

Danielle McCarthy (11)
The Brent Primary School

Christmas

C hildren play with the freezing snow
H appy people put up Christmas decorations
R ed roses start to appear at snow time
I ced car windscreens to scrape slowly
S hoes are freezing cold
T rees have lost their leaves in the cold winter's breeze
M erry Christmas to all the people in the world
A nd the people joyously celebrate Christmas
S inging children go around people's houses to entertain them.

Emily Thompson (9)
The Brent Primary School

Christmas

C old noses, where's the tissues?
H ot fire blazing light
R unny noses, get those tissues!
I cicle hanging from the rooftop
S lippery floor, people skidding
T winkling star glowing bright
M istletoe hanging from the roof, kissing everywhere
    around the house
A rctic ocean is an ice skating rink
S nowy days are excellent.

Robbie Underhill
The Brent Primary School

Christmas

C hoir singers on your doorstep
H aving fun in the frosty sunset
R abbits have their lovely sleep in the early winter's peak
I cicles are growing every second in the winter
S nowflakes are falling as the time goes by
T hermometers are moving down to freezing
M ist is getting thicker as the days go by
A rctic is getting absolutely freezing
S now is falling high from the sky.

Luke Newell (8)
The Brent Primary School

Christmas Poem

C lubs are closed on Christmas Day
H ats are woolly to keep us warm
R uby-red robins sing their songs
I gloo made out of ice bricks
S anta gives presents to everyone
T he boys and girls are asleep
M aking food for everyone to eat
A s the children are waiting for Father Christmas
S now is falling outside.

Marcel Wanstall (8)
The Brent Primary School

The Black Lion

I put on my swimsuit
Then round the corners I go
Down the steps into the light blue water.
The clasping cold wrapping me up in a blanket,
The air around me smells like mushy peas.
A few warm-ups to get warmer
And then
Off I go gliding through the clear glittery water.

Silky water brushing past my body
Everyone staring as I swim past
My cupped hands pushing the water away,
Suddenly
I swallow a bit of water
And it tastes like blood
Then to cool down I float along the turquoise water
Then I get out of the pool into my warm dolphin towel.

Krystal Matthews (9)
Twydall Junior School

Tidal Wave

The waves dash
While sparkling and filtering
The sun shines on the blue sea
Flowing through the raging current
Quickly or slowly, no one knows.

Now the water can't get through
A massive wall is in the way
Pushing and shoving as hard as it can
It flows in all directions.

A tidal wave comes into sight
It is coming straight towards me
No chance of escaping
I run and run and run . . .

Callum Duce (9)
Twydall Junior School

In The Loch

On the clear and luminous water
The sun shines down on the loch,
But within all the calmness,
In the secrets of the deep,
Something stirs.

The crabs vanish,
The scorpions crack
And the whales are brightening
In all their whitening
Yet still
Something stirs.

Underneath the rising
A cave shudders,
Carrying its cargo,
Bars of solid gold,
And silver crowns and bronze medals and
Brilliant copper coins,
Yet something stirs . . .
In the loch.

Benjamin Smith (9)
Twydall Junior School

The Drowning Water

The radiant surface whirls and twirls
against the clashing rocks.
Waving and swirling towards the cliff's edge.
Plunges down to the hollow
And battles the luminous water.
Gasping for air the bubbles float
just like a string of pearls
What is in the darkness?
Why is it so soft?
Down, down and down you go
Never to see the light again.

Amber Goddard (10)
Twydall Junior School

The Canal Tale

As I clamber on the boat so still
I look beyond and see only the shade of oak trees.
We go past lazy rocks so quiet,
Great muddy banks,
And a gentle flowing waterfall.

Then on every rock we see playful otters
Jumping on all the rocks around
Kingfishers darting down, down without a tiny ripple
To all the fish around,
But no human in sight.

Splish! Splash! Splosh!
Goes the only sound, the engine, so ghostly it sounds
I sweep my hands along some reeds, so dry, so very dry
What's that smell? Burning rubber?
Only the cars as we bump suddenly into the lock.

Up we rise to see the rest of this weird world
Along we go, currents pulling us along which could kill me,
Finally we harbour as water trickles down the small fall
Dad calls me along as I shoot
A last look at this deserted world.

Matthew Hurst (10)
Twydall Junior School

The Beach Of Paradise

There on the beach of paradise
I open up my eyes
to see a glistening bump
that lightens up the skies
then on the shining water
a dolphin reappears
jumping and splashing
it brings music to my ears.

Jessica Wood (10)
Twydall Junior School

The Watcher

In the lake below the silver mountain,
Do waters so luminous, bold,
Flow silently in the deep
Scaled fish swim
While pearly seaweed floats,
Near the bark.
Lots of sky-blue water
Pulse up from below,
As passing crabs are lost in puffs of sand.

The silver mountains reflection glows on the surface,
The clasping water is knawing on the side of the mountain,
While I watch endlessly on . . . forever.

Barnacles cling to rocks so raw,
No beauty such as the lakes have I seen,
Your banks tell a thousand tales
Look, a baby salmon,
Swims elegantly past my boat.

The silver mountains reflection glows on the surface,
The clasping water is knawing on the side of the mountain
While I watch endlessly on . . . forever.

Stelio Furner (10)
Twydall Junior School

The Glittering Lake

Shining droplets running through the cave
Clashing on the hollow stones
Echoing into the lake making splashing noises
Mesmerising through the bridges . . .

The surface breaks
A shiny helmet appears
The diver gasps for air
Then climbs out of the whirling pool . . .

Jasmine Randall (10)
Twydall Junior School

Nottinin Forest

We walk down
Nottinin Forest,
Starts to get windy,
Blowing and flowing,
Rain tumbling down,
Who's going to save us
In Nottinin Forest?

Drowning, drowning,
Can't even swim,
Who's going to save us
In Nottinin Forest?

Twister is appearing,
Going to eat us,
Twirling and whirling,
Getting closer,
Who's going to save us
In Nottinin Forest?

Me and my friends
Are getting scared,
No one to save us
Going to die.
Say a prayer, will it come true?
Who's going to save us
In Nottinin Forest?

Floods going down, twisters going down
My prayer came true, thank you God,
You saved us in Nottinin Forest.

Chantelle Wren (10)
Twydall Junior School

The Ocean

The waves that shine beyond the sea
beautiful colours shining back at me.
I look up and what do I see?
A bright waterfall shining at me.
The wind blows and it twists and twirls,
I watch it settle, the sight I see.
I touch the ocean,
It feels so cold,
My hands freeze
As the wind blows.
In my hands I caught something soft
A little dolly, a girl had lost.
I smell the sea salt with gifts for me
I hear the little girl shouting
Above the water so clean.
I think I'm so lucky
But not really
'Cause I'm talking to the ocean
While my friends can't see me.
I found a bottle in my pocket
I filled it with the ocean's water
I took it home and fell asleep
When I was sixteen I still had it.
That was the first time I had ever seen the ocean.
When I was an adult
I kept it in a safe place,
And every morning I'd wake
And remember the first day I had ever seen the ocean.

Chloe Ponsford (9)
Twydall Junior School

The Wonderful Waterfall Wanders . . .

The wonderful waterfall wanders around
Splashing and splishing it goes,
It hovers around the countryside,
Until it ends up low.

The wonderful waterfall wanders,
Splish! Splash! Splosh! it goes
Until it ends up nowhere
It dries up in the snow.

The other little droplets having fun at home
Making other droplets to play with them.

I wonder why water splashes on me?
All I hear are the silky waves
Crushing against the firm rocks.

I think I'm so lucky
But not really because all I hear is the water talking to me
I'm not sure if it's a miracle but let's go and see
If it is, it's a lovely thing anyway
But once I look up I see the sun setting
While the sparkling water lays under the glistening sunset which is
setting

I hear a song from a shell and I take it home
I fall asleep on my sofa in comfort.

Katie Haughton (10)
Twydall Junior School

The Sea

Over the sunken ships you flow
With raging waters swirling round and round continuously,
Your sparkling droplets fall when you clash into the rocks
Your shining violet torrents of radiant light glittering.
The raging whirlpool glistening, twirling and twisting,
Splashing and crashing against the rocks of the shore.

Michael Fegan (10)
Twydall Junior School

The Greatest Tap I Ever Used

Turquoise-blue wet water is splashing from the tap
And the sweet-tasting water rushes into the sink,
As I pour in a glass and lift up my cap
And I am relieved as I drink and drink . . .

I turn on the tap to splish in the bath,
And it is winter, it is pretty cold,
And Mum is outside, clearing the path,
I am dreaming, a story is told.

Now I am dirty,
I need a clean,
I squeeze a squirty toy,
The water is clean.

It came from the sea
Into a filter.
Now it is as safe as can be,
My fish have a filter.

Jack Stevens (9)
Twydall Junior School

A Cry

I see people crying
With a tear coming down
It's dripping like water just splashing down
The tears splash on the ground
With a quiet splash
The tears are bursting out
With a silent
Cry!

Ryan Barrett (10)
Twydall Junior School

Things Not To Do In The Swimming Pool

People are splashing in the gentle pool
Crying children with water in their eyes
Children playing games and having races.

People drowning and people saving them
People bringing them out the pool
Ambulance sirens going off trying to save.

The swimming pool may look safe
But all the time people are getting hurt,
So be careful what you do.

When you splash in the pool be careful
It will go in people's eyes,
So be careful when you splash.
The swimming pool is not what it seems.

Joshua Wheddon (10)
Twydall Junior School

The Snow

I woke up one morning
to see snow.
The cars were all covered in ice
and all the streets
were slippery.
All the dogs were jumping
and sniffing the snow
and all the children
were having snow fights.
Fox prints in the white street
and when I got home from school
I had a snowfight and then
a hot shower.

Alice Tappin (10)
Twydall Junior School

If There Was No Water

The stream running nearby
To the deep ocean
We all take it for granted,
But what if it were gone?

From the shallow end of a swimming pool,
To the deeper end,
We all use it for fun,
But what if it were gone?

In the bath tub,
Where we all get clean,
It may be all nice,
But what if it were gone?

When we put our hands under the tap,
To get them all clean,
We know we have to get the soap off,
But what if all the water was gone . . . forever?

If the water was all gone,
We would all be thirsty,
And all pass away,
But it will not happen from this day.

James McLuskie (10)
Twydall Junior School

Nasty Floods

As the river gets deeper
the floods get stronger
the rains get harder
then the river gets longer
and the people get more scared
as the boats get washed up on land.

Joshua Nicholls (9)
Twydall Junior School

Desperate For Water

A man walks through the Sahara
His thirst is unbearable
With lips sooty and a throat so red,
He walks on and on
He cries, 'Water, water!'
He's extremely desperate
But hope is near for an oasis is close
But no he collapses -
Dead on the ground.

David Lownds (10)
Twydall Junior School

Ice Cream

Ice cream is eaten at the seaside mostly
When it melts it dribbles all over your hand
It drips down onto the sand or rocks and turns into water
It sometimes colours the water, and slowly mixes into the sea,
To join the rest of the old ice cream again.
The water is then swallowed by fish and birds,
Then the fish are captured by the fishermen.

Molly-Jane Carter (9)
Twydall Junior School

The Starlit Stream

Flowing silver, bright and thin
the beautiful starlit stream whistles,
a faint melancholy sound.

But out of the distance
an elegant swan
of silver feather and crystal beak.
The waves of the stream suddenly danced
dampening each rock with their gentle splash.

Shanice Berko (10)
Twydall Junior School

I'm The River

I twist and turn
I spin and splash,
I wind through the riverbank,
I flow gently, I am the river.

Look over there,
Some cute little tadpoles,
They dart from pebble to pebble,
I flow gently, I am the river.

I gather the droplets
And other things,
Like geese and swans and tadpoles.

As I get closer and closer
To the exotic sea,
The current gets faster, wee!
Now I don't flow gently because I'm in the sea.

I bob up and down, up and down
With fish and stingray
Sea lions and otters and other things
I'm not the river anymore, I am the sea!

Sophie Aldridge (10)
Twydall Junior School

The Pond

The sparkling bubbling pond
My mesmerising tear
As the waving fish swim by
The smell is rising in the air.
The radiant stones are as cold as the wind.

It's like a silent dripping tap
In the middle of the night.
Drip, drip, drip
Flinging and flying the water.

Emma-Lea Millett (9)
Twydall Junior School

A Waterfall

When the waterfall threw itself off the cliffs,
It smashed, clashed and bashed on the rocks.
It went over and over again
Every year it goes through again.
Later on it was calm because it was on the rocks
It just disappeared.
It came into little pebbles.
Then the mermaids and mermen came too
It changed very quickly and oddly indeed
They were swimming everywhere,
They were looking at the place,
They were wandering everywhere, it was wonderful.

Ava Darby (9)
Twydall Junior School

Crystal Clear

My water's blue and ever so clear,
It can bring hate, love and fear.

I crash and smash around my large prison,
Bringing beauty and many visions.

My waters bring death and life,
The word comes to mind 'strife'.

My waters bounce off rock so white,
Your blood goes cold with that chilling bite.

So now on the banks of paradise my water's still . . .
I am crystal clear.

Scarlett-Jane Mann (9)
Twydall Junior School

The Wonderful Waterfall

When the water trickles through my hand, it feels like a sheet of silk
It's a wonderful sight to see in the sunset on a warm day,
It flows into the sea, I hear it every night just going everywhere,
The smell is perfect, it's just like lavender going through the air.

The wonderful waterfall splishing and splashing all night long,
Its fresh sparkling water going down the riverbank all ready to drink,
The wonderful waterfall so still and quiet, the sparkling wonderful
waterfall
Also quite lucky on the riverbank I sit happily as can be.

Shining, sparkling, whooshing, splashing, sploshing
Tasty little droplets on and on I see,
Dripping into the big ocean sea,
Makes my friends and me very happy.

Katie Stokes (9)
Twydall Junior School

The Stream

The stream is flowing down
Making a whizzing noise
Swirling and twirling as it works its way to the ocean
Crashing over rocks and boulders
No longer blue but white.

It sparkles like heavenly diamonds
And stars in the sky above
Rising and leaping, working with speed
Towards the open ocean.

Rebecca Coombs (10)
Twydall Junior School

Where's Wally?

I was walking down a path
Whilst I was having such a laugh
When all of a sudden
I saw jolly old Wally.

'I feel like I am still in bed
So let's play a game of hide-and-seek
To try and wake me up,' he said
'I hope you find me in this week.'

So I set off and was dripping wet from the rain
I had such a pain from a stitch from that wicked
old witch.

I looked in a house,
I looked in a marsh,
I looked at a mouse,
I looked quite harsh.

I looked under a spoon and thought,
What if he is on the moon?
And if he is, I think maybe he might be a ghost.

Jack Mullaney (11)
Warren Wood Primary School

Guess Who I Saw Today?

Guess who I saw today?
A gigantic shark.

Guess who I saw today?
Jackie Chan doing kung-fu.

Guess who I saw today?
A ferocious lion.

Guess who I saw today?
You.

Satveer Kaur (11)
Warren Wood Primary School

Fire

I start off as a little flicker
then I begin to grow,
you have no idea what I can do
until you see me glow.

I can burn down a house,
I can burn down a tree,
nobody can stop me.

So thank you very much
for your discarded match
because that's what made me hatch.

I can burn down a house
I can burn down a tree
Nobody can stop me!

Sam Waters (11)
Warren Wood Primary School

The Purple Flower

There was once a purple flower,
Who had a very cold shower.

She then went out walking
Met a friend and started talking.

She tripped and had a fall,
Got back up and sat on a wall.

The flower got up and went home,
Then sat on a chair and cried alone.

I'm so sorry but it's the end of the poem,
As I have got to do my sewing.

Jemma Parsons (10)
Warren Wood Primary School

The Cat And Mouse

In a house, in a wall,
Lives a mouse, very small,
The trouble is there is a cat,
Who likes to chase him around the mat.

Patiently by the hole,
Sits the mouse, happy soul.
Is the cat there? He looks,
Off with his head, it happens in books.

The mouse runs off
Cat chases after,
Cat in a room,
Stuck in the plaster.

The cat gets free
And catches the mouse,
Kick in the nose,
Mouse runs out.

Cat runs after
Dog chases cat
Mouse walks off
Mouse in laughter.

Rachel Amey-Drew (11)
Warren Wood Primary School

The Silly Billy Farmer

The silly billy farmer got up one rainy day
To get some stocky chicken
When a bird got in the way.
He got a little shotgun
Shot the birdie dead.
The bullet ricocheted
And got the farmer in the head.

Ryan Stanley (11)
Warren Wood Primary School

The Family

Grandmas and grandads telling stories,
Little kids are telling porkies.

Mum and Dad are watching the baby
The little kids are saying, 'Play with us maybe.'

The dogs are barking and sniffing round
But the cats are nowhere to be found.

The kids are laughing
The baby's crying.

The kids are being naughty
With the dog called Sporty.

The kids are laughing
The pets are moving,
The baby's crying,
While the time is passing.

Francis Carey (10)
Warren Wood Primary School

The Man-Eating Loo

I was sitting on the loo
What am I going to do?
The toilet pulled me in
It made an awful din
I don't know where I landed
But I was totally surrounded
I was trying to climb out
When I heard someone shout
Finally I got out then
And I never went back again.

Perry Morgan (11)
Warren Wood Primary School

The Tree Of Seasons

In the deepest part of the forest
Is a tree
But this is no ordinary tree.

Through spring and summer
It stands tall
In autumn and winter
It's quite small.

In winter comes the forester
Chops down the tree
And leaves no splinters.

But back in spring
He's reborn
To his old self
The tree of the seasons.

Peter Cole (11)
Warren Wood Primary School

Rotten Rat

Rotten rat, rotten rat
With your smelly rotten teeth
Rotten rat, rotten rat,
Getting everyone in grief
Rotten rat, rotten rat
Running through the town
Rotten rat, rotten rat
He nicked my dressing gown
Rotten rat, rotten rat
Come up the toilet bend
Rotten rat, rotten rat
I was cleaning my rear end.

Shayla Sutcliffe (10)
Warren Wood Primary School

My Birthday Party

It was my birthday party,
Everybody came,
It was at my house,
The adults would now be tame.

All my friends came,
Peter, Rachel, Jake,
My nan was also coming too,
But she fell over a rake.

Lots and lots of presents,
Piling on the stair,
Someone even told me,
They got me a great white hare!

Once everyone was inside,
And my dad slammed the door,
I started opening presents,
Sitting on the floor.

After I had finished,
We all ate some cake,
Then everyone left,
Leaving bad smells in their wake!

Thomas Williams (11)
Warren Wood Primary School

Dragon

D id you hear that
R apid winds fly past?
A bout to flatten everything
G oing far and wide
O ut its cave to our homes
N o I heard a lovely dragon flying over the trees.

Ashleigh Patrick (10)
Warren Wood Primary School

War

In the barren wastelands
Something's going on
War and fighting and a merry song.

Infantry and commanders,
Fighting side by side
Arrows fly swiftly and on the cavalry ride.

Merciful people die,
For their proud country,
Soldiers cry but still they try,
They know they'll be lucky to survive.

Side by side they fall,
Silence fills the air,
Men begin to crawl, the enemy do not care.

Victory is here,
Home is near,
For those who survived the trip,
Will give the enemy the slip.

Jake Shannon (11)
Warren Wood Primary School

There Was A Girl On The Bus

There was a girl on the bus,
So I made a great big fuss.

I asked if she wanted to dance,
She said, 'Tonight' with a lovely glance.

I asked her where she lived,
She said, 'Near where you live.'

She said, 'Where shall we go?'
I said, 'Somewhere with fake snow.'

We met down at the restaurant,
And she was standing right in front.

Connor Anderson (11)
Warren Wood Primary School

Did You Know?

Did you know if you're too close to the TV
You get square eyes?

Did you know if you eat too many sweets
You'll turn into one?

Did you know if you eat all your carrots
You can see in the dark?

Did you know if you poke yourself with a pencil
You'll get lead poisoning?

Did you know when you pull funny faces
And the wind changes, you stay like that?

Did you know that these are stories
Made up by your parents?

Hannah Burt (10)
Warren Wood Primary School

Evil And Dark

E xtreme caution is needed
V ile creatures are feeded
I n underground caves
L ive dark, evil slaves

A nonymous figures are on the drapes
N asty villains in dark capes
D evilish people in contorted shapes

D emons with fiery tridents burn
A nybody shall burn to an urn
R avenous creatures with sharp claws
K illing creepy things with strong jaws.

William Packwood (10)
Warren Wood Primary School

There's A Monster In The Spare Room

There's a monster in the spare room
We feed it bread and tea,
There's a monster in the spare room,
It roars and growls at me.

There's a monster in the spare room,
Which Mum says is our kith and kin,
There's a monster in the spare room,
It's got a thorn bush on its chin.

There's a monster in the spare room,
Which stares through big round eyes,
There's a monster in the spare room,
Which Dad says it nearly dies.

There's a monster in the spare room,
It gave me a present,
There wasn't a monster in the spare room -
It was my grandad!

James Tutt (11)
Warren Wood Primary School

Santa Claus

Santa Claus has got big paws
Santa Claus can get through doors
Santa Claus on pies he gnaws
Santa Claus above clouds he soars
Santa Claus the weather he ignores
Santa Claus delivering presents and flying
                              are his chores.

Michael Olsen (10)
Warren Wood Primary School

Crazy Caterpillars

Come take a look and see what I've found
Crazy little caterpillars all over the ground
Hairy ones, stripy ones, and ones with spots,
Green ones, black ones, ones with bright yellow dots.

These crazy caterpillars, glorious green,
And on leaves the same shade, they can hardly be seen.
Brown prickly ones hides on a twig,
Can you see him, is he little or big?

These crazy caterpillars are a hungry bunch,
They nibble on plants, for breakfast and lunch.
They nibble and nibble and nibble some more
On scrumptious green leaves
They love and adore.

No longer hungry and needing a sleep
Along the branches the caterpillars creep,
It's time now to spin some silky cocoons,
And snuggle inside for a nice long snooze.

Hannah Cates (10)
Warren Wood Primary School

Valentines

Valentines, Valentines,
Showing all your love,
Valentines, Valentines,
As sweet as a feathered dove,
Valentines, Valentines,
From deep within your heart,
Valentines, Valentines,
Which love makes very smart.

Calvin Costen (10)
Warren Wood Primary School

What's Wrong With Me?

Wandering home to get my tea,
the same old question bothered me.
The ladybird she laughed at me
I asked her, 'Why?'
She said, 'I must fly.'
I asked the cricket, 'Why do they laugh?'
He hopped off saying, 'Don't ask me.'
I asked the dog, 'What's wrong with me?'
He barked saying, 'I must rush, I've got a flea.'
In desperation I asked the ants,
They sniggered, 'Your skirt, it's tucked in your pants!'

Laura Colley (11)
Warren Wood Primary School

Humpty Dumpty

Humpty Dumpty sat on a tree
Humpty Dumpty broke his knee
He went to the doctor and guess what Humpty said?
He said he'd broken his knee instead of his head.
'What should I do? I know, go straight to bed.'
Humpty Dumpty went back home and asked for tea.
His mum said, 'Who wants a doughnut?'
'Not me!'

Jamee Salam (11)
Warren Wood Primary School